BETTER PHOTOGRAPHY FOR AMATEURS

A MODERN PHOTOGUIDE

BETTER PHOTOGRAPHY FOR AMATEURS

by

D. X. Fenten

AMPHOTO
Garden City, New York 11530

PREFACE

Few of us enjoy remaining static throughout our lives. We want excitement, variety, and improvement. Amateur photographers are no exception, rather they are outstanding examples, always striving for something better, photographically. Not written as a basic text on photography, this book is specifically aimed at the amateur who knows something about photography, and has taken many photos, some good, but most not so good. It is written by an amateur photographer, and in many cases, illustrated by amateur photographers, so that other amateur photographers can see and learn from mutual experiences.

Every author fervently hopes his work will affect readers deeply. We only desire that photographers will use this book as a stepping-stone to more fun, creativity, and enjoyment through better photography.

The author gratefully acknowledges the photos and information so generously contributed by the leading photographic manufacturers and suppliers. Special thanks to friends and associates whose suggestions, photos, and help made this book possible. To my wife, Barbara, eternal thanks and love for everything, which now includes editing and typing assistance.

D. X. Fenten

CONTENTS

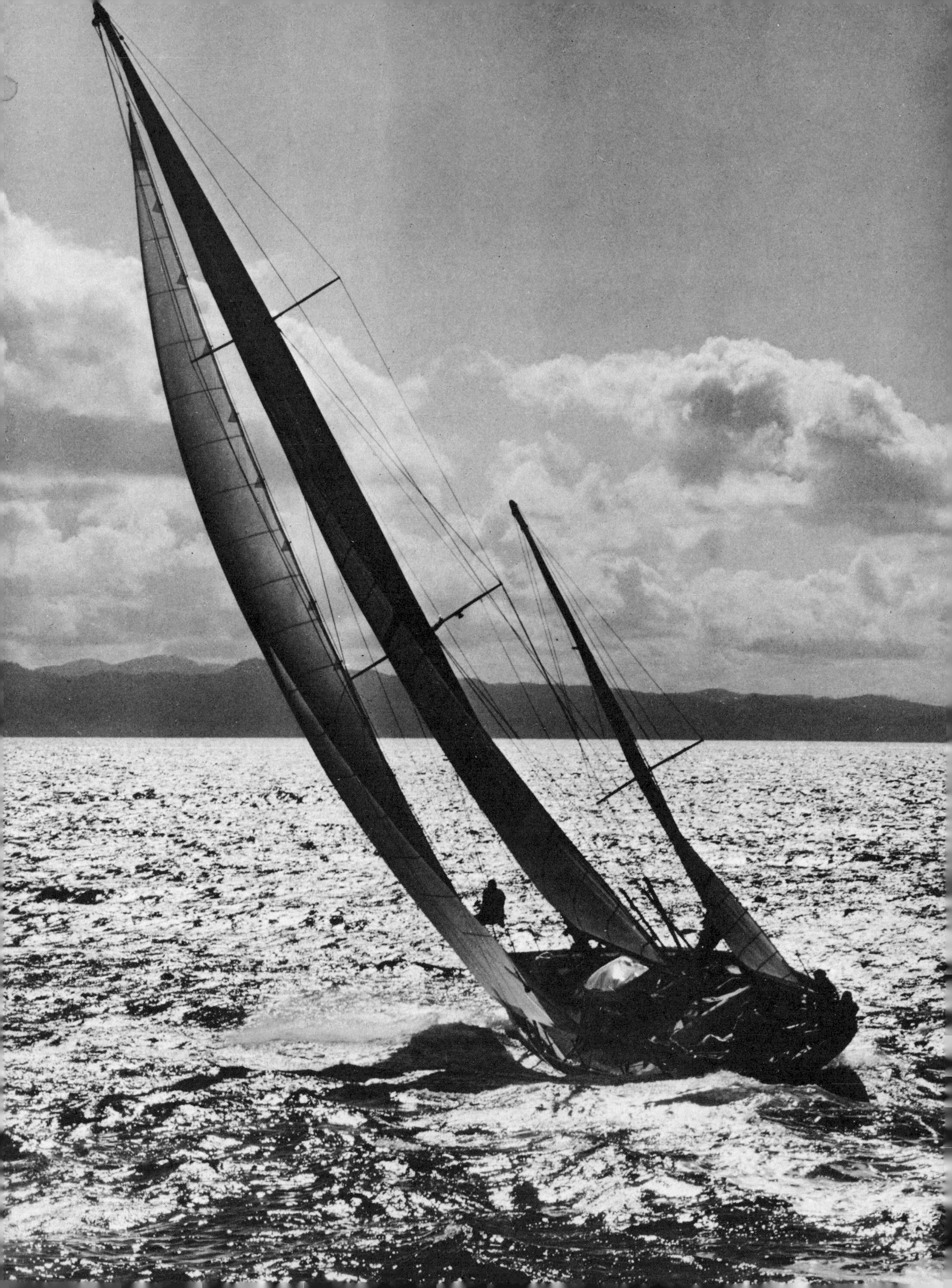

1

GOOD PHOTOS ARE MADE...
THEY DON'T JUST HAPPEN

Leonardo started it all. He noticed that a small hole drilled in a room or building could cause the formation, on the wall facing the hole, of an upside-down image of an illuminated scene outside the room. Da Vinci didn't know it, but he was describing the first pinhole camera, *camera obscura* ("dark room").

Since the portability of a full-sized room was questionable, someone had to come to Leonardo's aid. Without knowing of da Vinci's discovery, Giambattista della Porta, at 15, clearly presented the *camera obscura* and later introduced a concave mirror for producing the image. Though room-sized cameras were in use in his lifetime, della Porta is credited with making the portable camera possible.

Now that a reasonably sized camera was available, and this as early as the fifteenth century, more complications were added. The image, once formed, had to be retained. Johann Heinrich Schulze, in 1725, started the photographic ball rolling by discovering that the darkening of silver salts was the result of light, and not heat, as had been believed. Giacomo Battista Beccarius took it a step further in 1757 when he found that silver chloride was sensitive to light, allowing the production of image designs on materials like bone and marble.

From here on in, everything was downhill. They had the da Vinci–della Porta camera, and a light-sensitive medium for image retention. Further refinements encompassed the creative inventiveness of Thomas Wedgwood, Joseph Priestley, and Sir Humphry Davy. Joseph Nicéphore Niépce, credited with making the first photograph on a light-sensitive material within a camera, teamed with Louis Daguerre to improve photographic methods. The Niépce work, carried on by his son, produced the soon-to-become-world-famous daguerreotypes.

Photography got its name in 1839, when Sir John Herschel used the term. For the next 50 years, photographers the world over improved equipment, techniques, and sciences of photography. But the art of photography did not stand still while science advanced. While the scientists persevered, the artists experimented.

The experiments resulted in notable photographs by T. H. O'Sullivan, Alexander Gardner, Vandiveer Hayden; early action photos were made by Eadweard Muybridge, Thomas Eakins, and Jules Marey. A bit later, stereoscopic photography, currently enjoying a revival, became popular. In the 1850's, photographers became considerably more concerned with photography as an art form than simply as a form of recording, so portraiture, architectural, and landscape photography flourished. Throughout the Civil War, Mathew Brady and his staff made thousands of photos, many destined for immortality. Later still came the pioneers of photography as an art: Alfred Stieglitz and Edward Steichen. So, while all manner of improvement was being made on the technical and scientific front, the actual artistic part of picture taking kept pace.

During all this time, however, photography was not for the amateur. The equipment was too complicated, too expensive, too bulky—simply too much for the amateur. The year 1884 marked the beginning of the end of the barriers to popular photography. In that year, George Eastman introduced a roll film consisting of a paper coated with a silver-bromide emulsion.

Boating Westward. Photo by Eric Scott.

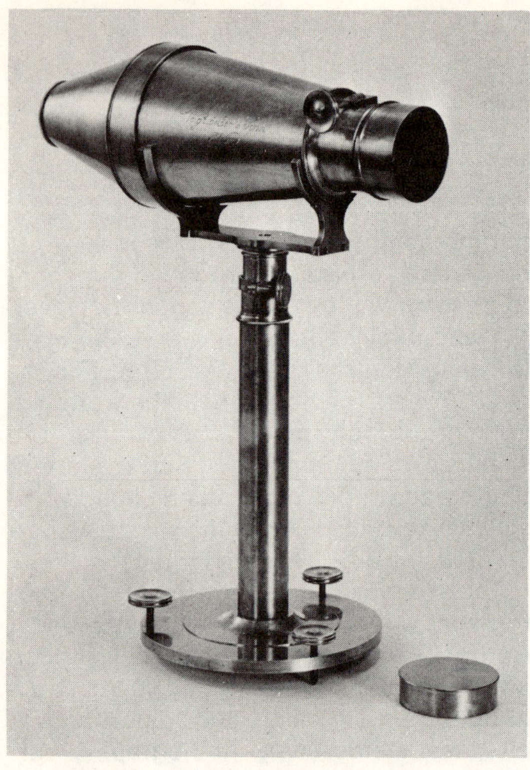

First all-metal camera. Produced in 1840 by Voigtländer A.G.

Four years later, transparent nitrocellulose replaced paper as the base for film. Shortly thereafter, Eastman completed his simplification of photography with the introduction and manufacture of the first compact roll-film camera. The cameras, Kodaks, began what can be considered the modern era in photography. For, with the introduction of these simple, compact, inexpensive, easily operated cameras, anyone could take a photograph . . . and almost everyone did, or so it seemed.

Since the introduction of the first roll-film cameras and the simple snapshot box cameras, many hundreds of millions of photographs have been taken by amateurs. No matter how kind one tries to be, the great majority of these photos must be classified as lackluster, mediocre, or just plain bad. Surely this description has fit many of your shots, just as it has mine.

It is a bit difficult to understand how the amateur photographer can spend so much time, money, and effort and still get relatively poor results. Perhaps we have been snowed under by an avalanche of ultra-fine equipment, which cannot make up for our deficiencies. Or, perhaps we are quite satisfied to sit back and hope our cameras, from the most inexpensive box camera to the Leicas, Nikons, and the like, will come with built-in intelligence, ingenuity, inspiration, and imagination. Please don't wait. They just cannot make this type of camera. Although the electric-eye cameras solve many problems, the greater part of the burden still rests on you, the photographer.

Learn to make the most of what you have, and from this, plus your experience and that of other amateurs and professionals, learn to take better photographs.

As we all know, photography's basic ingredients are: a camera, film, subject, and light. Everybody, professional or amateur, starts off with these four basics. The difference is what you do with them. Despite the great divergence in equipment, cost, and complexity, it is the amateur or professional who thinks photographically that gets the better shots. Thinking photographically includes many things, but to most photographers it means, high on the list, the proper care and maintenance of camera and equipment.

EQUIPMENT—CARE AND MAINTENANCE

The photographer's tool is the camera. As with any tool, the most admirable results are obtained from one that has been properly cared for and faithfully maintained. Since cameras are precision instruments and are, as such, unable to withstand abuse, special care must be taken.

Before setting out on a shooting spree, check your equipment carefully. There is nothing quite so frustrating as discovering, upon developing a roll of film, that something wrong in the camera has ruined every picture. Upon checking the camera, if something seems to be wrong, such as a sticking shutter or an out-of-kilter synchronizer, take it to a camera repairman. He will check it, lubricate it, and repair anything out of order. Finally, he will test it for you. Don't try to monkey with the camera yourself, for you will most surely do irreparable harm. It is a good idea to have your camera checked periodically by an authorized repairman. Logical times for these checkups are just before your summer vacation and before Christmas.

Though it is not wise for the amateur to attempt to repair or tinker with a camera, there are several things he can do to care for and prolong the life of his camera. Always keep your camera in a case; the "everready," front-opening types are most convenient. While a case will not take the place of careful handling, it will protect the camera from most bumps and bangs as well as sand and dust.

To further protect your camera, guard one of its most important parts, the lens. Always keep a lens cap on the lens when it is not in use. Never leave a camera with the lens pointed up in the sun. A short time in this position under a hot sun, and your lens will be ruined. This is especially true of the very fine lenses, those that are coated and color corrected. It is also wise never to store a camera in the glove compartment of a car. The heat that builds up in a closed compartment of this type can become intense enough to cause serious damage.

Both the lens and the inside of your camera must be kept clean to insure best performance. To remove dust and lint from a lens or the inside of a camera, use a brush, preferably a blower-brush combination specifically made for this purpose. Do *not* use a handkerchief, shirt tail, tie end, or any

Typical Mathew Brady Civil War photograph reproduced from the original negative. Photo courtesy of National Archives.

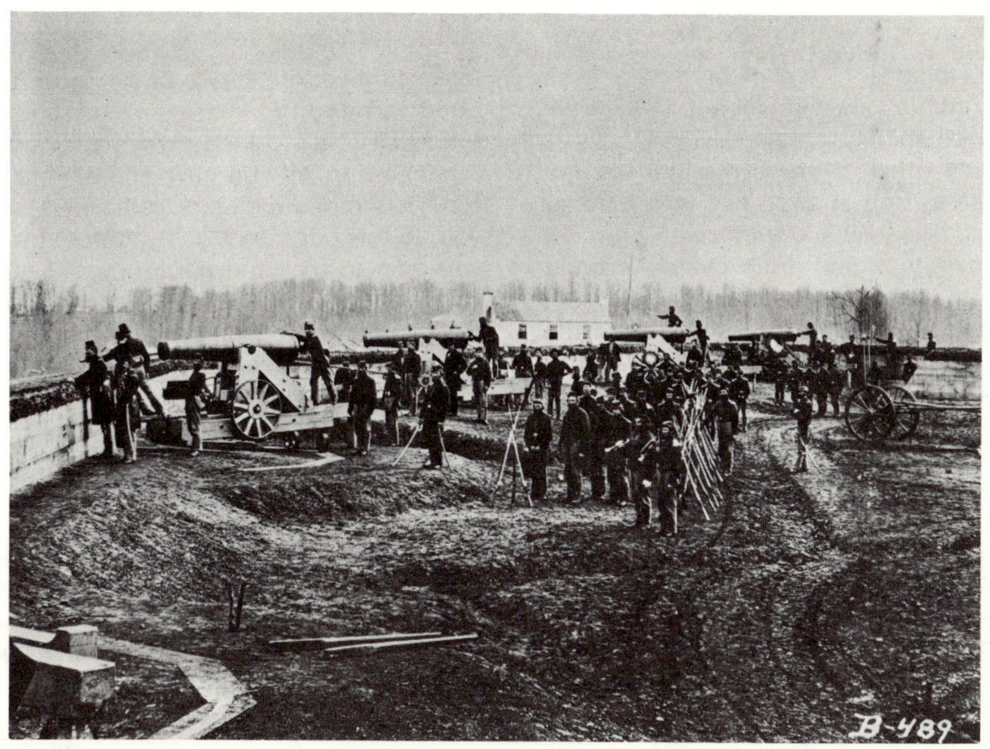

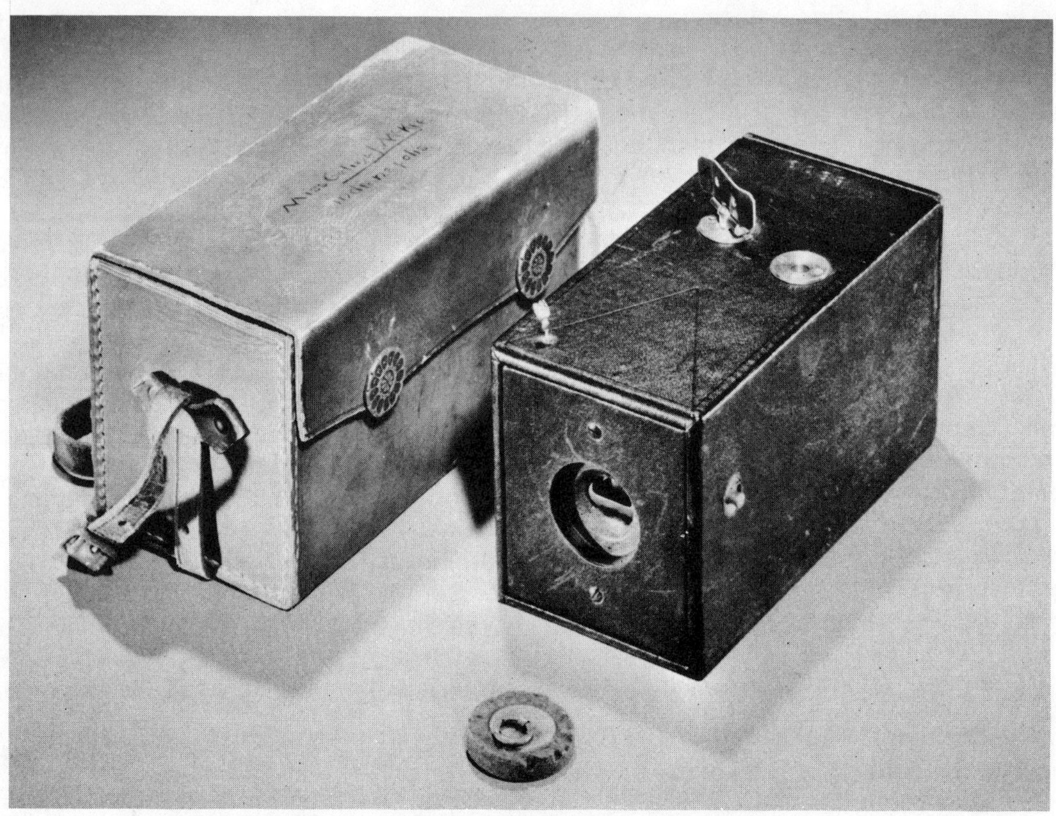

(Above) First compact roll-film camera, the Kodak, which began the modern era in photography in 1888, and (right) photo taken with this camera. Photos courtesy of Eastman Kodak.

other "available" piece of cloth, as these may scratch a lens and will definitely leave more lint than they remove.

For any other cleaning required by the lens, use a drop of approved lens cleaner and lens tissue. Wipe the lens with a gentle, circular motion, and don't overdo a good thing. In handling the camera for use, cleaning, or anything else, make sure the fingers are kept away from the lens. A greasy fingerprint on a lens will show up beautifully on a photograph. Unlike your eye which will compensate somewhat for dirty eyeglass lenses, the camera records exactly what it sees, and makes no allowances for your carelessness.

Your camera is not the only piece of equipment which requires care and periodic maintenance. Before a shooting session, make sure your flashgun or strobe unit is in good working order. Be sure the batteries are fresh and working properly. Check all other equipment you have and plan to use: tripods, exposure meters, self-timers, etc. If you do this conscientiously, before the day you plan to take the photographs, and all your equipment is clean and in proper working condition, a good portion of the battle for better photos will have been won.

FILM VARIETY

Today's amateur often has it too good. The great variety of films available seems to cover every conceivable shooting situation, but often, this very variety serves only to confuse and makes proper selection diffi-

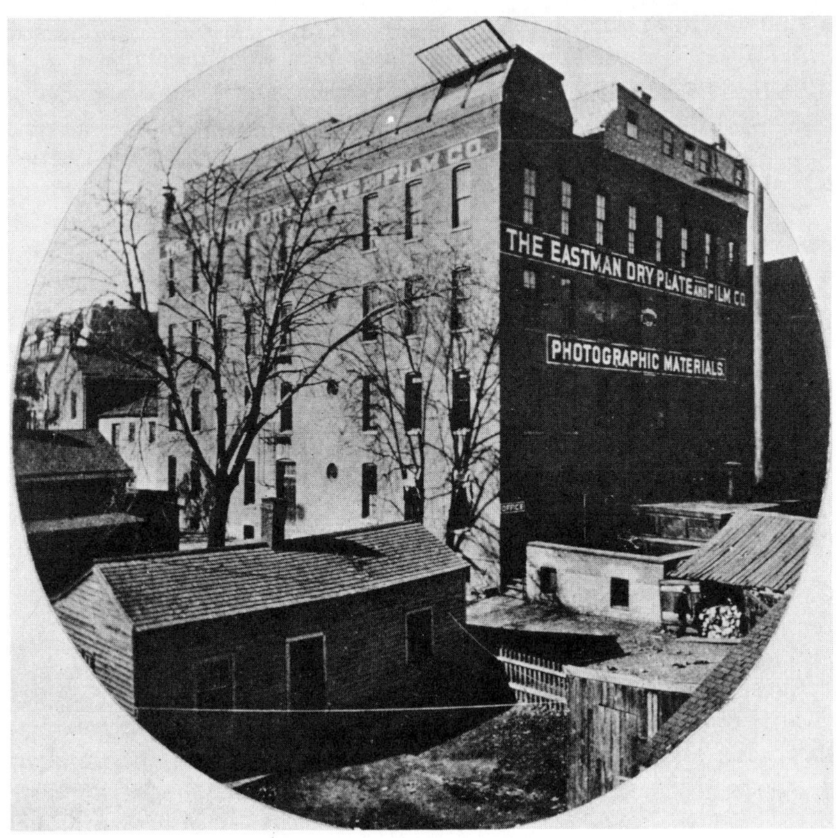

cult. The questions regarding which film, for what, why, and how usually provide the greatest confusion. A more detailed explanation of available films, their properties and uses, will follow in Chapter 3; meanwhile, let it suffice to say, take along plenty, in a variety of speeds.

A safe rule to follow when preparing for a shooting session is to decide approximately what you expect to photograph, estimate the lighting conditions, and, with these things in mind, select the *slowest* film suitable. The slower the film, the finer the grain. This is especially important if you intend to enlarge small negatives, such as 35mm, to 8″ x 10″, 11″ x 14″, or more. One further caution—take enough film and shoot more than enough. Film is one of the least expensive items in photography, considerably cheaper than a fleeting expression or special picture you miss because you're out of film.

SAME SUBJECT, BETTER PHOTOS

Just about anyone can take photos. All one has to do is load a camera with film, aim, push the button, and the deed is done. The big question is whether the button is pushed with or without forethought. To get better photographs, to lift yourself out of the class of lens clickers, who depend solely upon a mood of the moment, subject to nothing more than a whim or fancy, plus a little luck, follow a few very simple rules about the subject of your picture-taking.

First, make sure you have a good reason for taking a photograph. Remember, you will look at this picture again and again. Make sure the reason for having taken it is apparent to both you and anyone else who may be viewing it. If the photograph must be studied to try and figure out why it was taken, it is a poor picture.

Then, try to capture exactly the mood and idea you intend to portray. This will be explained more fully in Chapter 5, but for now, keep the idea of picture mood or feeling in mind.

Finally, make each subject in your photo a complete unit, with as few distracting elements as possible. Make only a single point important in each photo, and be sure to focus attention carefully on this single area. This can be achieved by attending to such things as subject arrangement, background, and camera angle. When handled correctly, all these things contribute to completeness in a photograph and make for considerably better photos.

WITHOUT LIGHT ... NOTHING

Taking pictures requires light. Getting better photographs requires, among other things, that *you* control the light and make it work for you. It is light that controls each photograph as you take it, develop it, and ultimately show it. That is, the light has control, unless you control the light. Better photos can be made only if you acquire a working knowledge of light, and what it can do. You must then use this knowledge to get the light to do what you want it to do, and go where you want it to go.

There are aids to the correct use of the light you already have: exposure meters and exposure guides. There are also ways to create new or additional light: flashbulbs and cubes, electronic flashes, and floodlights. While each of these will be discussed at length in a later chapter, it should be noted here that, as with anything else, knowledge put to use will make the difference between mediocrity and near perfection. With light the most important ingredient of photography, since a photograph is merely a light picture, it is correct usage and control that make the difference.

STARTING OFF RIGHT

Quality in photography often depends upon experience. The beginner may get very fine photos the first time out, and then rest on these "laurels" and never improve. If he is interested in getting better photos, he takes many hundreds of photos, looks for, and learns from his mistakes, learns from others, masters his tools, and then, combining all, he begins to get consistently better photographs. The first attribute must be the desire to get better photographs. If the photographer has this, he must then get confidence, information, and the knowledge of his tools. His camera tops the list of tools.

2

A RELIABLE CAMERA IS YOUR BEST TOOL

No camera is any better than the photographer who uses it. The most advanced, expensive, gadget-laden camera is no better than an elementary, inexpensive box camera until someone uses it well. Despite the cravings of most amateurs for the latest up-to-date camera models, it is probably true that the best camera for the amateur is the one he owns and knows how to use. The sooner we accept the fact that the photographer and not the camera is responsible for good, bad, and indifferent photos, the faster progress can be made toward better photographs.

Cameras differ in size, speed, and specialty. On these differences, and of course quality, rest camera costs. Take your own camera, for example, and compare it with the most inexpensive and simple box camera. Are there many, or any, basic differences? Both cameras are boxes which keep out all light except that which is allowed to enter through the lens when the shutter is open. Each has a lens which, despite size, shape, quality, and cost, is specifically designed to focus rays of light to form a sharp image on a strip of film. The similarity continues with the shutter. Every camera has some mechanical means, either metal leaf or slit curtain, of allowing light in for a determined amount of time. The film must be moved up to prevent more than one exposure on a single frame of film, so all cameras have a film-advance device. To complete the similarity, all cameras allow the photographer to see what he is taking, so a viewer is standard equipment on all cameras. Naturally, this explanation is over-simplified, but the point it proves is true—no matter the camera, or its cost, all cameras are basically alike, and fine photographs are quite possible with any of them.

As the cost and complexity of a camera move upward, gadgets and versatility increase proportionately. The previous discussion should not be used as an argument against the purchase of new or additional cameras and equipment. Rather, it aims to stimulate each photographer to get better photographs from the equipment he now has. Further discussion and explanation of each of the popular camera types—box, folding, 35mm, single-lens reflex, twin-lens reflex, view and press, and Polaroid Land—with emphasis on their advantages and disadvantages, capabilities and specialties, should whet the appetite of every photographer. It should either make him more determined to get better photos with the camera he has, or send him to the nearest camera store for a bigger and better camera.

BOX AND SIMPLE CAMERAS

The "box" camera is the simplest, easiest camera to operate. It gives the photographer little, if any, choice of lens opening, speed, or depth of field. The photographer loads the camera, aims it, pushes a button, and he has taken a picture. Until recently, box cameras could only be used if conditions were excellent. However, most modern box-type cameras have integral flash-holders, flashcube mounts, or even electronically programmed shutters. As a result, pictures can now be taken indoors or outdoors, under most conditions. To add even more to the flexibility of these heretofore totally inflexible box cameras, medium and fast films are readily available in both color and black-and-white. In fact, the modern cartridge-loading 126-size, and newer "pocket" 110-size, simple cameras have come a long way toward the capabilities of their more sophisticated counterparts. There are few real "box" cameras left.

The major disadvantages of the simplest cameras are few, but important. Box cameras lack versatility, forcing the photographer to operate with a permanently fixed shutter speed and lens opening. In addition, the simple lens cannot be expected to be on a par with the more complicated, many-element lenses in regard to sharpness.

In defense of the simple camera, one may say that if more amateur photographers took their "basic training" with such inexpensive cameras, their pictures would be better, and they would save a considerable amount of money. The box camera can be operated by anyone, even children, and is ideal for youngsters since its rugged construction and simple mechanism make it almost indestructible. Pictures taken six feet or more from the subject will be quite clear from this distance to infinity. This should be kept in mind when a background is being considered. To evaluate the simple cameras, they can be considered wonderful beginning tools, especially for youngsters, and can be used to take good pictures with the barest minimum of photographic knowledge by a maximum number of people.

FOLDING CAMERAS

Though few of these once-popular cameras are still available new, the number of used models for sale—and in everyday use —remains great, for the wide variety of folding cameras makes them a breed unto themselves. Just as some folding cameras are little more than box cameras that fold, others are precision instruments capable of the utmost in quality and versatility.

The inexpensive folding cameras, on a price level with box cameras, offer little besides the compactness gained from folding. Though these cameras have a bellows, it adds little to the camera's capability, with the exception of lens focusing by scale.

High-priced folding cameras incorporate just about everything a photographer could ever desire—interchangeable lenses, coupled rangefinders, camera movements such as tilts and swings to eliminate distortion, bellows attachments for close-up work, and of course, flash and strobe synchronization. However, photographers must pay for their heart's desires—many folding cameras were quite expensive new, and remain so, even used.

The main disadvantages of the average medium-priced folding camera include non-interchangeable lenses, possibility of bellows damage causing light leaks, and no parallax compensation or correction when taking close-ups. However, these are offset by the camera's advantages. Because they usually use roll film, 620 or 120 size, folding cameras make excellent snapshot cameras. These easily operated cameras give large-size negatives, which are excellent for enlargements and are even big enough for satisfactory contact prints. Of course, there

Kodak Pocket Instamatics are smaller than ever. Only 1″ thick, they produce 3½″ x 4½″ snapshots.

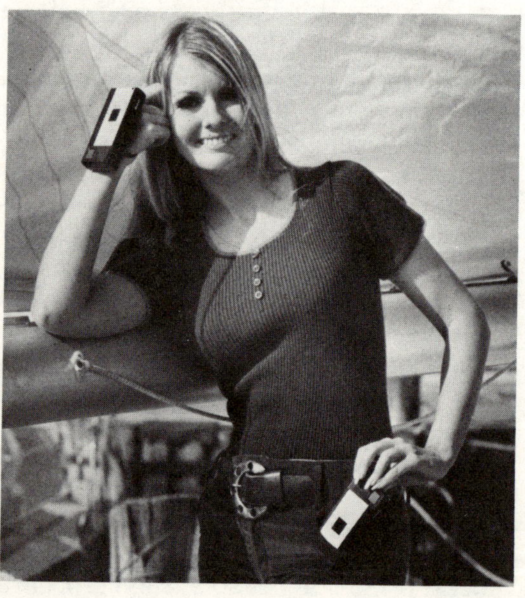

is a bit more to remember, manipulate, and adjust when using a folding camera than when using a box camera. These adjustments of diaphragm opening, distance scale, and lens speed are relatively simple and require little more than care and experience.

To get better pictures with a folding camera, make use of each of its added features —and be sure to check each before every exposure. Some experts recommend that the camera be set at f/16, 1/50 sec., which is very close to the presettings on a box camera, so you can get used to the camera when first using it. This is not as good an idea as getting used to the camera the right way—the way the camera was meant to be used. If you teach yourself to use each of the adjustments on the camera from the very start, it will soon become second nature to you. Then, you will be able to begin experimenting, making these adjustments work to your advantage, to capture the correct mood, expression, background, and composition of each photo.

35MM CAMERAS

Among the most popular and fastest-selling cameras on the market are the 35mm miniatures, although the term "miniature" is rarely used today. Call them what you will, they offer such tremendous advantages over other types of cameras that they are used for virtually every task, including many situations considered taboo for small film not long ago.

Small, compact, and unobtrusive, the 35mm's are true candid cameras. Since most have short-focal-length lenses, usually 50mm, they offer almost incredible depth of field. This can be used to great advantage in candid photography, allowing the photographer to get many "one chance only" shots without worrying about precise focusing.

Simpler 35mm cameras focus by scale and have limited shutter-speed and lens options. More complex models use range-

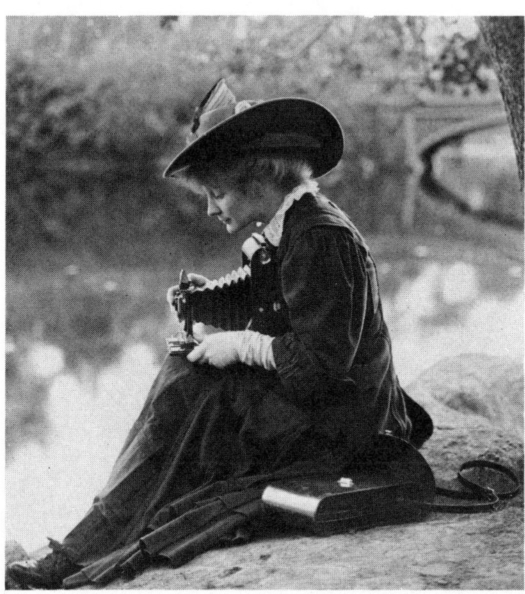

We've come a long way since the era of the huge folding camera and the huge folding dress.

finders to focus and have a wider range of shutter speeds and lens apertures. The finest of the rangefinder 35's have such advanced features as built-in metering, exposure automation, and even lens interchangeability. In recent years, however, the single-lens reflex, as described below, has taken over the market for premium 35mm cameras.

Adding to the ever growing popularity of the miniature cameras is their low operating cost. This does not mean 35mm cameras are inexpensive when purchased. They are, for the most part, precision photographic instruments, and are priced accordingly. They do, however, offer a very low cost per picture, in either black-and-white or color.

While on the subject of 35mm film, it should be noted that the relative ease of making fine color slides for showing in a projector also accounts for some of the popularity of these versatile cameras. The color slides, when returned from the processor all mounted and ready to go, can

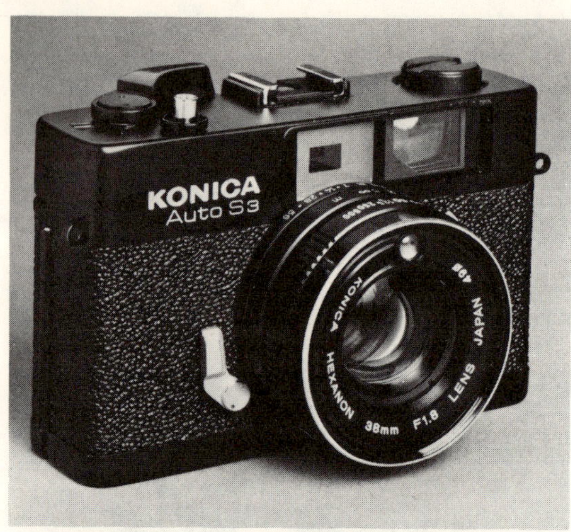

Rangefinder 35mm cameras are small, sophisticated, and easy to use. Some have electric-eye automatic exposure systems, and a few still require an exposure meter reading.

become breathtaking when shown at home on a large screen. In addition to this capability, the 35mm cameras also offer black-and-white negative film in speeds far beyond those required by most amateurs.

Naturally, the miniatures, despite the great number of advantages, also pose several important drawbacks. The very advantage of small camera size becomes a problem when negative size is considered. With the exception of color slide film, all other film used must be greatly enlarged to amount to anything. It is common to blow up the 1″ x 1½″ 35mm negative to 8″ x 10″, 11″ x 14″, or even larger prints. However, some loss of sharpness should be expected unless the exposure, development, and enlargement have been flawless. The smallest bit of dust or lint, or the tiniest scratch becomes formidable when enlarged ten or fifteen times.

SINGLE-LENS REFLEX CAMERAS

Single-lens reflex cameras use almost every film size, and so have the advantages and disadvantages attached to the various film sizes. The biggest advantage of the single-lens reflex camera is the fact that you get exactly what you see. That is, no matter the lens used or the distance from the subject, whatever you see on the groundglass viewer will appear on the film. This is possible and practical because single-lens reflex cameras utilize the same lens for viewing and picture-taking.

Utilizing this feature, single-lens reflex cameras are fine for all picture situations suited to miniature cameras, and are especially suited to extreme close-ups. A mirror reflects the image seen by the lens onto a negative-size groundglass, and you focus, compose, and get exactly what you see. This differs from the rangefinder 35's, for with these, a small portion of what is seen in the viewfinder does not appear on the film, owing to the slight difference in position of the viewfinder from the lens. This difference is called "parallax."

To a great extent single-lens reflex 35mm cameras have replaced rangefinder cameras in the hands and hearts of both amateur and professional photographers. They are available in price ranges from the sublime to the ridiculous. For a time, some of these cameras, notably the least expensive ones, were handicapped by the viewing arrangement. In dim light, or when the lens had been shut down a bit, the image was difficult to see. Today's models have automatic diaphragms, which remain open while you compose and focus and shut down to the preset opening as the mirror flips out of the way, just a split second after you have released the shutter.

These extremely versatile cameras have an unbelievable array of accessories available. Most have telephoto, wide-angle, close-up, and zoom lenses, and some have motor drives. All of this makes the single-lens reflex cameras just about perfect for any picture-taking situation. Then, add the elimination of the parallax problem, and you have the camera many photographers believe is ideal.

SINGLE-FRAME CAMERAS

Between regular 35mm cameras and the ultraminiature (16mm) are the popular single-frame cameras (18 x 24mm). Using standard 35mm film cassettes, these light-weight, compact cameras give twice as many exposures for each roll—40 exposures on a 20-exposure roll, 72 shots on a roll of 36-exposure film. Almost all have electric-eye exposure systems, simplified focusing, and are horizontally held, giving a vertical photo. Coupling film economy with simplicity, accuracy, and carrying and operating ease, the single-frame cameras have long been popular.

TWIN-LENS REFLEX CAMERAS

The twin-lens reflex cameras differ considerably, especially in appearance, from their single-lens cousins. While most single-lens reflexes look very much like other 35mm cameras, the twin-lens group looks like a reflex should, like the first such camera, the Rolleiflex.

As their name implies, these cameras have two separate lenses, one for composing and viewing, the other for actually taking the picture. In addition to viewing and composing through this special lens, you also use it for focusing. Located just above the picture-taking lens, the viewing lens reflects the scene onto a groundglass, allowing you to see the scene and then to focus directly on the groundglass. To assure the utmost in sharpness, most cameras include a small magnifying glass so a small portion of the picture on the groundglass can be checked for clarity and pinpoint sharpness.

Maximum flexibility of format is offered by these cameras, since their 2¼″ x 2¼″ pictures eliminate the horizontal versus vertical problem encountered with rectangular film sizes. To add further versatility to some of these cameras, special adapters allow up to five different picture sizes and shapes, as well as a choice of between 12 and 24 exposures from a single roll of film.

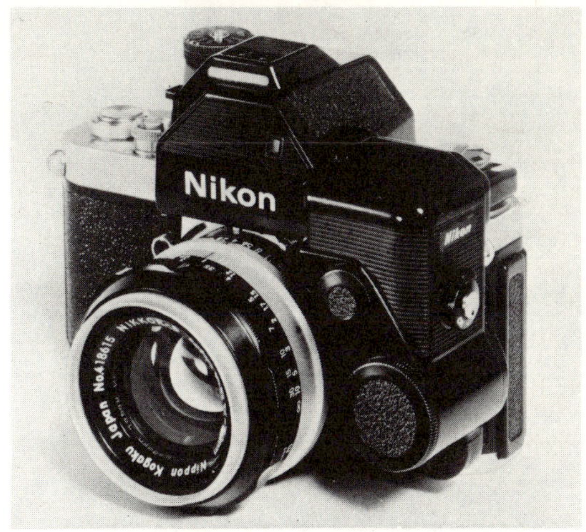

This very sophisticated, relatively expensive single-lens reflex camera has just about everything a photographer could want. And if it is not built-in, it comes as an accessory.

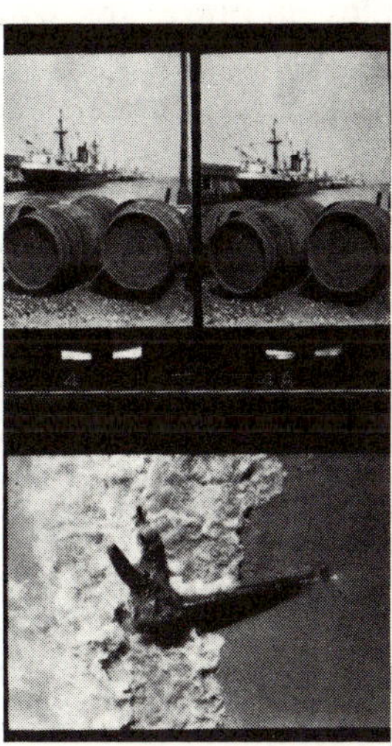

Single frame and standard 35mm negatives are compared in this photo. Normal 36-exposure roll of 35mm film yields 72 single-frame photos.

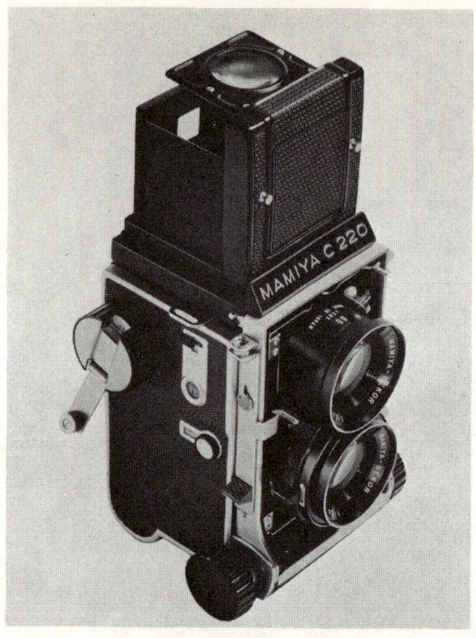

This Mamiya twin-lens reflex is favored by many photographers. Its advantages include film size, shape, and unmatched camera reliability.

With these adapters, good-sized black-and-white enlargements as well as color slides for projection are possible. These cameras all eliminate the slight blackout encountered in some single-lens cameras when the mirror flips up out of the way. You see the scene you are taking before, during, and after tripping the shutter.

Though not specifically designed for candid or action photography, arrangements have been made to make these situations a bit easier and more accurate with the reflex cameras. If, however, most of your picture-taking is going to be of the candid or action type, these cameras are less than ideal for your purpose.

Another of the major disadvantages of these twin-lens reflex cameras is that non-interchangeability of lenses remains in all but a few models. As a result, unless you can afford one of the cameras with interchangeable lenses, you must rely on the lens in the camera for all work. This eliminates the telephoto and wide-angle lenses from your bag of camera tricks.

Many professionals swear by these cameras, and their reliability easily warrants this confidence. So, despite any inconveniences and disadvantages, the reflex cameras are often the standard camera of both professional and amateur.

ULTRAMINIATURE CAMERAS

Characterized by their smaller-than-cigarette-pack size, the ultraminiature cameras tend to remind one of espionage work. However, the models on the market are quite legitimate in intention, and offer features equal to those of larger cameras—fast lenses, flash synchronization, 50-exposure film cartridges, and a full line of accessories. Especially fine for candid work, where the photographer must not look as if he is taking a picture or even carrying a camera, these tiny instruments are capable of producing high-quality reproduction. The latest "Pocket" 110-size cameras, though listed here as simple cameras, are in this category.

Utilizing many different film sizes, usually cut down from branded film and specially spooled into magazines, these cameras most often give negatives approximately 16mm wide. While the film size makes perfect exposure and processing a must, normal jumbo prints are quite good, and even larger prints are possible.

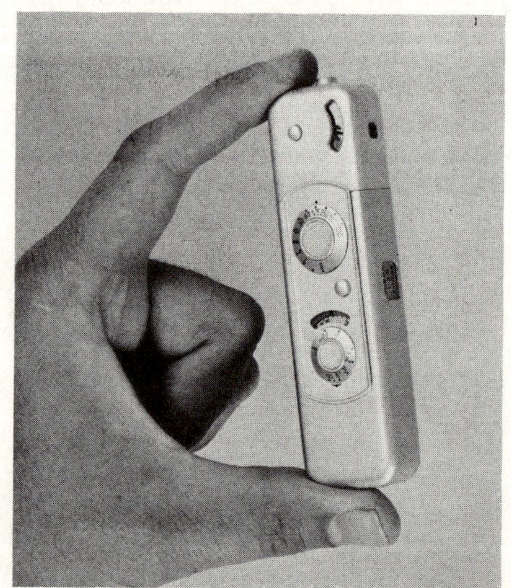

The Minox, the best known of all the ultraminiature cameras, can be used in all situations, including those in which a "normal" camera might be obtrusive.

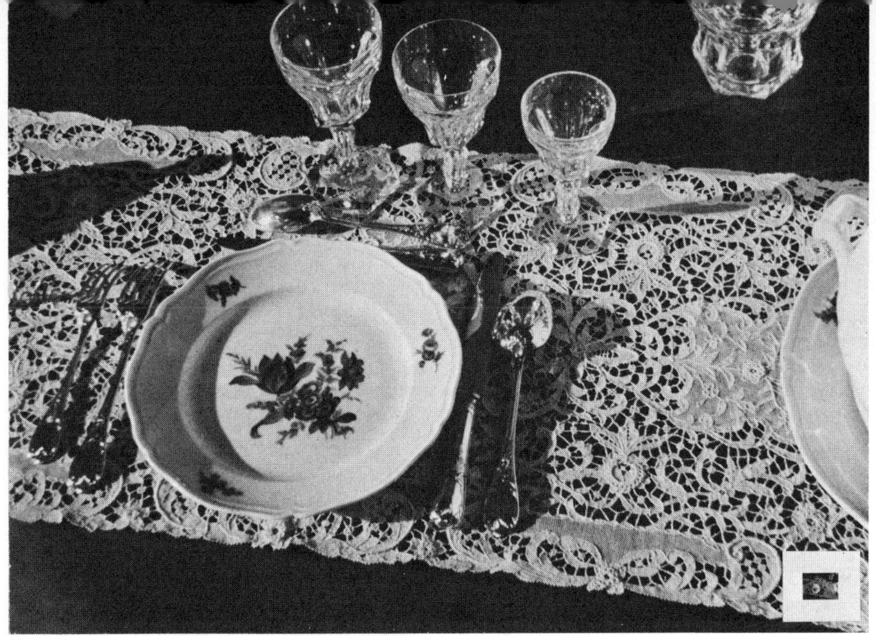

Enlargement from 16mm ultraminiature, with negative shown in proportion. Photo courtesy of GaMi.

VIEW AND PRESS CAMERAS

Despite the fact that view and press cameras are the most versatile, give the largest negative, have camera movement provided by tilting lenses and bellows, and provide pinpoint sharpness and detail, they are not normally used by the amateur, because of their large size and relatively expensive film. Most popular with news photographers, studio photographers, and industrial photographers who must have the detail provided by large negatives that will not be lost through enlarging, they include every feature any photographer might want.

These cameras can do anything, and do it perfectly. Either a sportsfinder or ground-glass is used for composing and focusing, and interchangeable lenses up to astronomical size are available. These are truly professional instruments.

POLAROID LAND CAMERAS

Ten seconds after you have snapped the shutter, you have a permanent black-and-white print. Sixty seconds after you have snapped the shutter, you have a permanent color print. Need much more be said about the "instant photography" Polaroid Land cameras?

As always, there is considerably more to say about the Polaroid Land system. Now there is another brand-new camera/film system, the SX-70. With it, the film is ejected from the camera 1.5 seconds after you press the button. The picture ($3^{1}/_{8}''$ x $3^{1}/_{8}''$) appears by itself out of the front of the camera. It is hard, dry, and brilliantly shiny. You need do nothing. Nothing to peel apart, nothing to throw away. Everything is automatic. All you do is sit back and watch. In a very few minutes the color picture is developed fully, even in brightest daylight. When completed, the photos are durable and can be handled, stacked, and thoroughly enjoyed.

It is no wonder that this revolutionary photographic system has gained such unprecedented popularity in the short time it has been available. It is quite safe to say this photographic revolution, the greatest in almost 75 years, is here to stay.

Photography, as we knew it before the Polaroid Land cameras, consisted of three steps after the exposure had been made—developing the negative, exposing a positive by using the developed negative, and then developing the positive. Today, the Polaroid cameras combine all three steps into one, taking just 10 seconds for black-and-white.

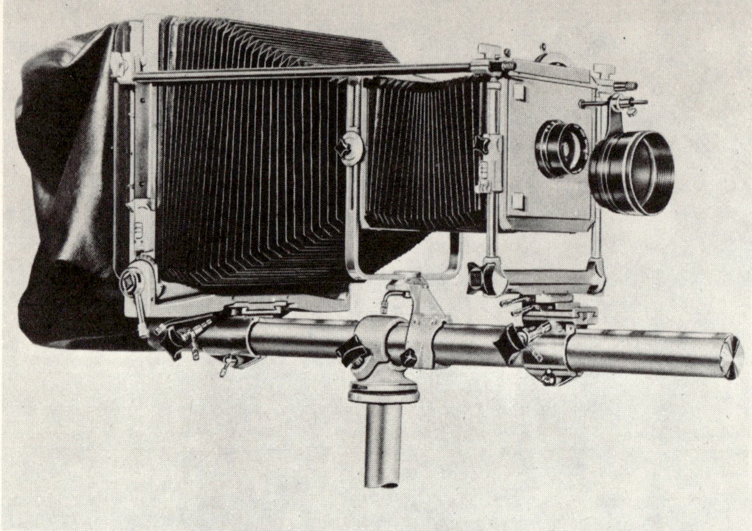

Sinar View camera provides tilts, swings, and anything else a photographer might desire.

Because the Polaroid cameras are extremely simple to operate and require no technical developing skill is no reason to feel that these remarkable cameras are toys or require no photographic skill. A poorly exposed, focused, or composed picture will be just as bad if taken with a Polaroid as it would be if taken with any other camera. By the same token, excellent photos can be taken with the Polaroid. Many professionals now include them as "must" items with their other photographic equipment.

The picture-in-a-minute cameras offer many rather obvious advantages to the photographer. First and foremost, with this camera you have a second chance. A photo not as good as you wished can be retaken just a minute later (while the jam is still on the face, or the kitten still has the ball of yarn), with the result immediately comparable with the original. Of course, a good photographer should not have to rely on this hit-or-miss method. Instead, by heeding the rules applicable to conventional cameras, and adding a few special ones for these special cameras, the first shot and every shot will count.

As we have already discussed, conventional cameras must be kept free of dust and dirt. Polaroid cameras require this and special cleaning attention. Since developing solutions are spread entirely within the camera, the possibility of developer leaking from between the negative and positive is great. If this is allowed to harden, chances are quite good it will ruin at least several photos. A damp cloth will easily remove developer while it is soft or sticky—but after it has hardened, you must chip or scrape it off with a fingernail and then use a soft, damp cloth. Dirt marks, white spots, and uneven developing result from dirty camera backs and rollers.

Become thoroughly familiar with the procedure for pulling the tab and film through the camera. A smooth, firm pull is best; otherwise, many faults will appear on your Polaroid prints.

Though Polaroid color prints need no coating, some black-and-white films require an even, unstreaked plastic coating. When using the coater supplied for black-and-white prints, move it only in a single direction. While the prints are drying, keep them apart, and free of dirt and dust. Any specks of dirt or dust falling on the wet plastic will permanently mar the print. The newest Polaroid black-and-white prints require no coating.

Since most Polaroid Land photos are meant to be used the same size they come from the camera (though fine enlargements are available inexpensively from the Polaroid Enlargement Service), make the most of the large film size. Get close to your subject—not close enough so parallax becomes a problem—but close enough so the element or elements being photographed

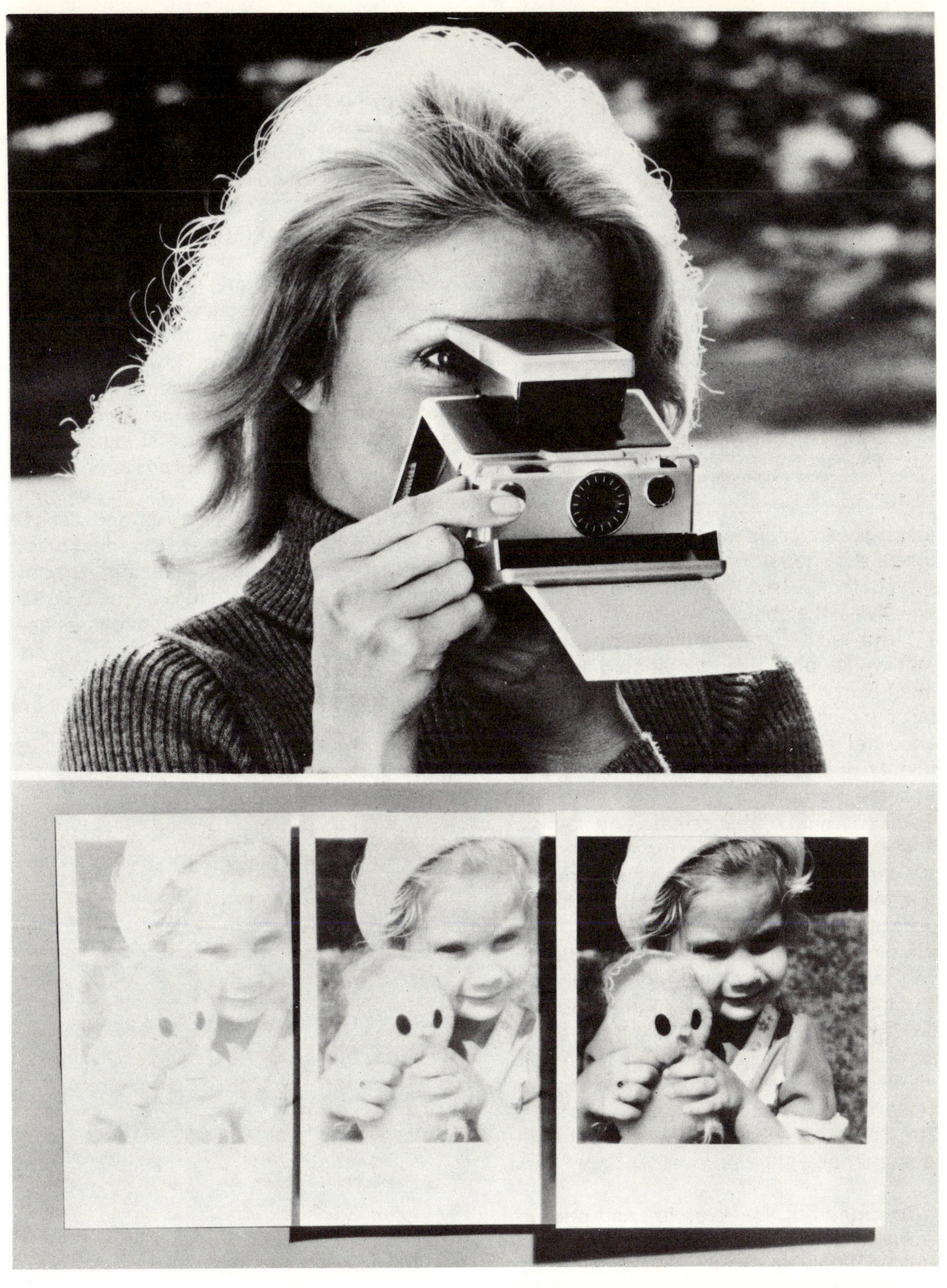

*The Polaroid SX-70 camera shows the way
photos look as they develop outside the camera.*

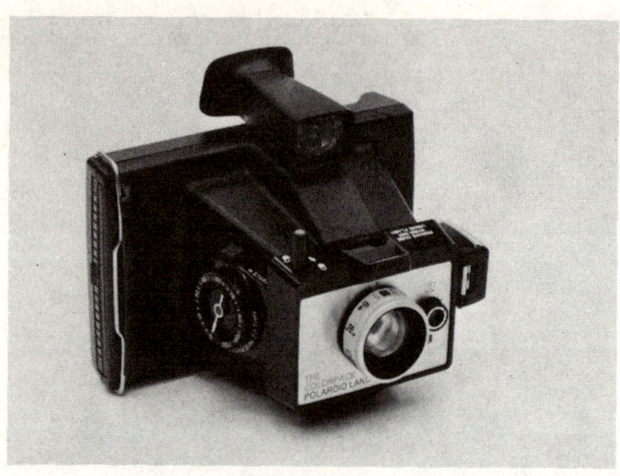

Polaroid Colorpack camera is simple to use, inexpensive, and it incorporates many features found on more expensive equipment.

are a good size, filling up most of the picture area. The larger and better composed the subject matter appears, the more impressive is the photo.

These are but a few of the special considerations a photographer should keep in mind when using the Polaroid cameras. Couple these with background and experience gained taking pictures with conventional cameras, and you are almost assured of better pictures.

A discussion of this camera and its revolutionary system would be incomplete without mention of some of its equally revolutionary, specially designed materials and accessories.

Most of the Polaroid camera models can be used with a complete range of films, including Polacolor and the high-speed ASA 3000 film. The high-speed black-and-white film allows you to get good photo results under just about any lighting conditions. Flash cubes, magicubes, and Focused Flash units add just the right amount of instantaneous light wherever you may need it.

To round out the Polaroid Land photography system, there are special films for making black-and-white photographs and a special film that gives you both a black-and-white print and negative, without a darkroom, in just 30 seconds. There are al-

so copying stands, close-up lens kits, filter sets, and other items that make this whole new world of photography one of the most exciting to open up in many years.

ALL KINDS OF CAMERAS

To summarize, there are cameras to fit every need, pocketbook, and degree of proficiency. The best camera for the amateur is the one which he knows how to handle. If he is going to buy a new camera, he should not be dazzled by gadgets, claims, or clever advertising. Instead, he should shop around, decide for what purposes he wants to use his camera, and find the camera which best suits his purposes and needs. He should have this camera demonstrated, handle it himself, and after buying it, learn everything he can about it. He should be so accustomed to using it that it becomes another working part—an extension—of his own eyes.

To make the most of any camera, once he has learned all there is about the mechanics of the camera itself, the photographer must go one step further in making his camera work for him. He must experiment with the different films available. This endless variety helps make photography as fascinating as it is.

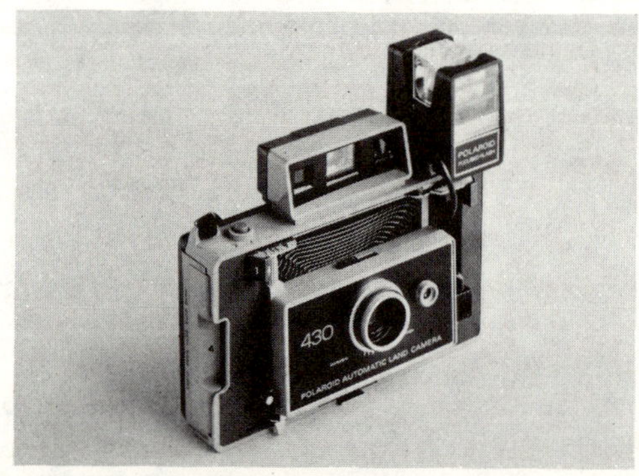

This Polaroid camera features a Focused Flash system that couples to the rangefinder of the camera and precisely regulates the amount of light reaching the subject as the user focuses the camera.

3

CORRECT FILM FOR EVERY OCCASION

The recording element of any camera, indeed of photography, is a very thin sheet of plastic, covered with a gelatinized emulsion of light-sensitive silver chemicals—film. Since film must record accurately under widely diversified conditions, there must, of necessity, be a wide variety of films on the market, suited for general use and special situations. There are black-and-white as well as color, negative and slide, ultra-high speed, fine grain, orthochromatic and panchromatic, to mention just a few.

You must decide for what purpose the film is to be used, whether graininess will be a problem, the expected lighting conditions under which the film will be exposed, and the subject to be photographed. In short, you must know what you are doing, or rather, what you are going to do, before you select the film to do the job. Most simply, you could consult a chart, such as the one shown later in this chapter. This is merely a starter. Instead, learn about film and the various film types before selecting one for a particular situation. Even after you have made your selection, you still have a bit of leeway, and your knowledge of films and their sensitivities permits certain interpretations of film rules and regulations.

FILM SPEED

Assume that you have already determined the film size that correctly fits your camera. If there are any doubts, return with it to your photo dealer, to verify the proper film size. You are now set to choose the right film speed for your shooting situation. Film speed is determined by the manufacturer, according to a system set by the American Standards Association (ASA). This film speed can be found on the information sheet packed with every roll of film. Listed as either E.I. (exposure index) number or ASA number, this film-speed rating should be used as your guide number for exposure. Some cameras and films use German (DIN) film-speed numbers. These can be identified as low numbers up to the twenties, while the more widely used ASA numbers range from the twenties to the thousands. Whatever system you choose, check your camera against the film instruction sheet, and use a single system throughout.

GRAIN

To gain the terrifically high speeds desired by some today, something must be sacrificed. In many cases it is fine grain. As the speed of the film increases, so does the graininess, proportionately. Though large-sized enlargements can be achieved with a minimum of noticeable grain from super-fast films, grain does become apparent when, for instance, a small portion of a 35mm negative is used for a very large-sized enlargement, 11" x 14", or 16" x 20". If you expect to make enlargements of this size, stick to the medium-speed films, and grain will not be a problem.

BLACK-AND-WHITE FILM

There are probably as many different black-and-white films presently available as there are situations in which they could be used, and photographically, situations are almost limitless. It stands to reason, there-

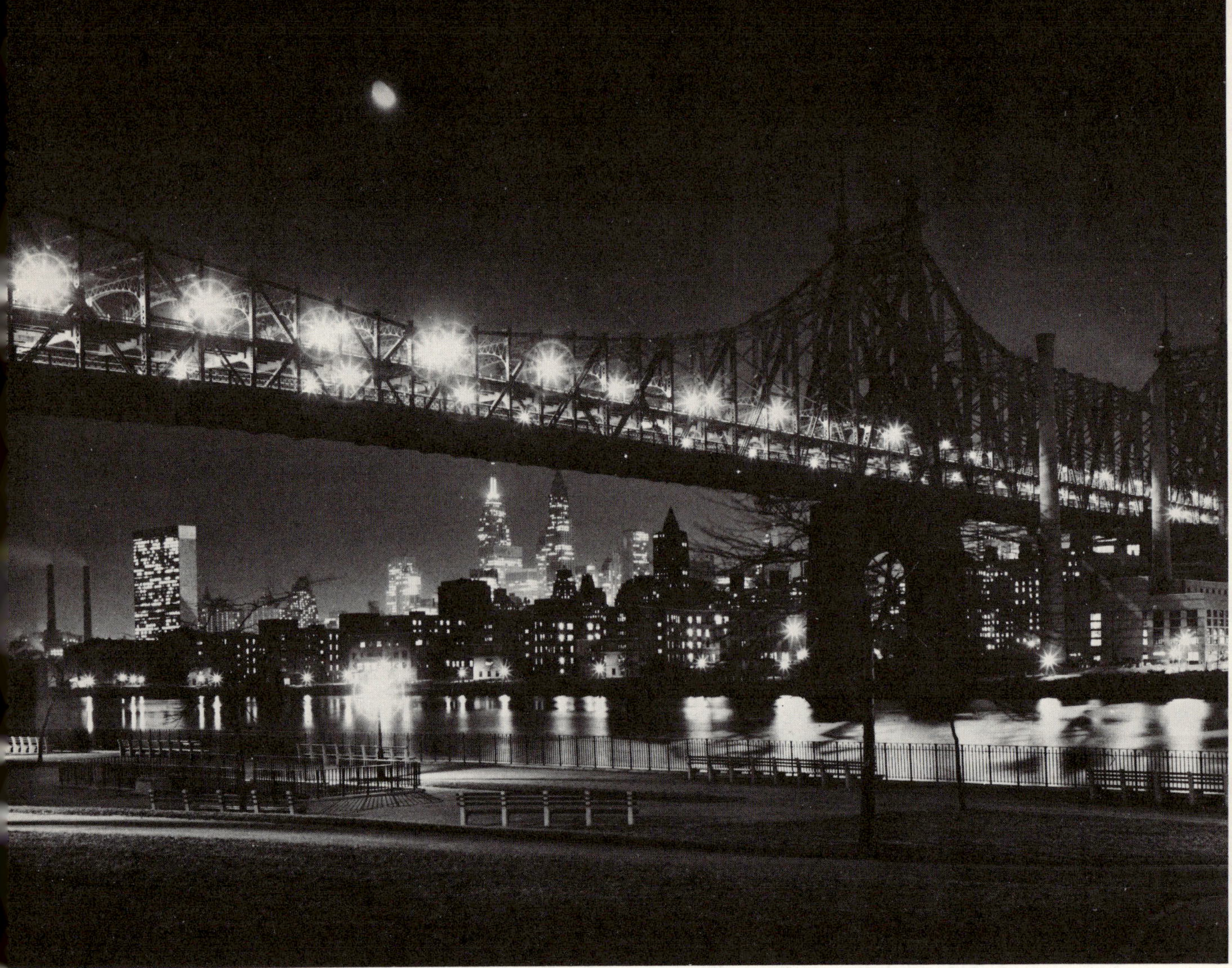

Magic Lights. Photo by Frederick E. Annette.

fore, that selecting a film, especially for a particular situation, will help to do the very best job possible, certainly a better job than a film not suited for the situation. Select the right film. Do not depend upon the versatility of modern films to adapt to your situation. The closer you get to the ideal film per situation, the closer you are to getting better photographs.

The two basic types of black-and-white film are panchromatic and orthochromatic. While most film used today is of the pan type, there remain many uses for and users of orthochromatic films. Panchromatic films are sensitive to all parts of the spec-trum, rendering a faithful, wide range of tones in blacks, greys, and whites for each color seen. These films should be used for all general-purpose photography. Ortho-chromatic films should be reserved for special situations. They are sensitive to just about all parts of the spectrum except red, to which they are almost totally blind. As a result, reds come out black, and the relatively small gray range yields a very high-contrast photo. For strong character portraits of men and to hold the pink cheeks in baby portraits, orthochromatic film is recommended—however, pan film should be used for virtually everything else.

26

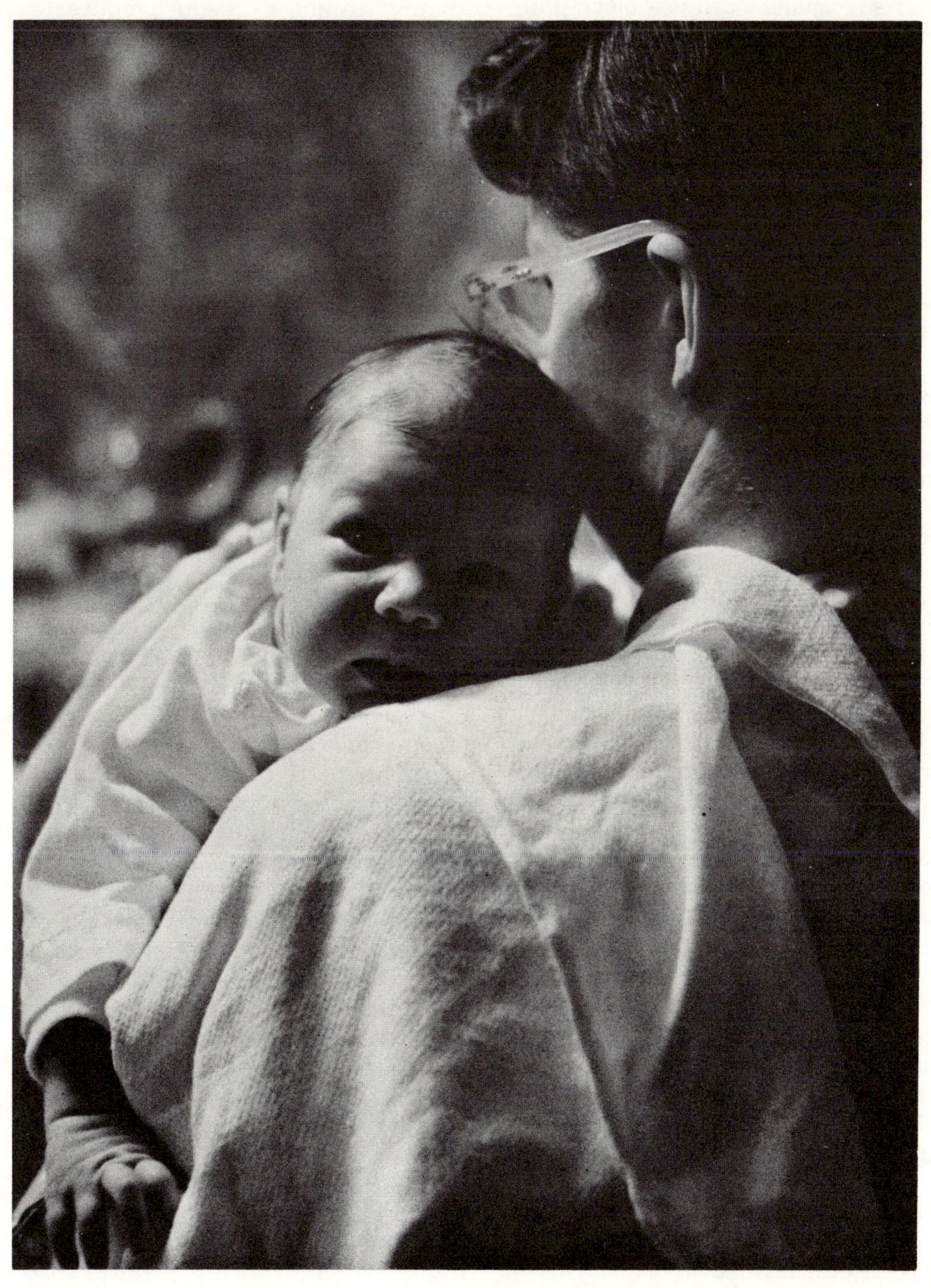

*Photo taken under available light conditions
with Nikon and Plux-X film. DXF.*

COLOR FILM

Just as any amateur can use black-and-white films to produce creditable prints, he can also do extremely well with color film. While it is true most amateurs cannot develop and print color material as they can black-and-white (though it is becoming increasingly simple), it is also true that all the basic rules of photography apply. However, with color one must be a little more careful.

The two different kinds of color films, transparency (or reversal) film and negative film, serve overlapping purposes today. The transparency films produce positives (slides) through which light passes to give us a picture. Negative films provide a negative from which a paper print is made. Today, with many transparency films, you can have fine paper prints and enlargements made directly from the transparency. Similarly, negative film can now be used not only for print making but also for slide transparencies. However, these secondary capabilities should be used only as reserve assets. Color reversal film should be used to make slides, and the negative films should be used where paper prints and enlargements are the primary desire.

As previously mentioned, color film requires the photographer to be more careful than if he were using black-and-white. This is because there is not as much latitude with color films. Even slight over- or underexposure will show up on a color positive, appearing as off-true-color rendition. For this reason, exact readings must be taken from an exposure meter and accurately transferred to shutter speeds and lens openings.

Unlike black-and-white films, in which contrasts are made in brightness and darkness, color film contrasts are actually made in color. So, where flat lighting gives a dull, unappealing photo with black-and-white film, it is the best bet for color film.

Color film is delicately balanced for use under certain lighting conditions—either sunlight photos taken at midday or with strong artificial light. Daylight film should be exposed between the so-called midday hours, as later exposure produces a definite reddish tint to the photo. Indoor films, for tungsten or flash, if used outdoors, will give a heavy blue tint to a photo. With the help of blue flashbulbs, various filters, and combinations, either type of color film can be used, in an emergency, for either type of light. Electronic flash, the artificial light most like sunlight, can be used indoors or out with color film. There is no appreciable color rendition penalty when using strobe units with daylight films.

To get better color pictures, be they slides, prints, or large transparencies, great care and accuracy must be taken. The film types produced by different manufacturers vary in color rendition, as can two films made by the same company, so try them all, and use the one that most appeals to you.

When using color film, search out the nuances of color, for these slight shadings and tone differences will be recorded by the delicately balanced color film and make for beautiful results. Another point to remember for improving your color shots is color consciousness. When taking a picture, be aware of the colors present, and think of how they will look on a screen. Do not have too many color-contrast extremes, for this will tend to make your slides look like a three-ring circus. The colors will vie for importance, and your subject will be completely overlooked. Instead, use color to your advantage by having soft, appealing colors highlight the subject. Color for color's sake quickly becomes tiresome, but color used to contribute to a composition means better and more beautiful color photographs.

CORRECT FILM FOR BETTER PHOTOS

To round out the information previously given, several additional items concerning film selection will help you get better negatives, and as a result, better prints.

Always select the slowest film possible to do the specific job at hand. The slower the film, the fewer the problems. With the slower films, grain is usually negligible, the image is sharper, developing is faster and easier, and in general, your chances for good photos are better.

Though it is a good idea to experiment with many of the fine films available, it is also a good idea to use one kind of film for a long time, or at least until you are thoroughly familiar with its characteristics and capabilities. By that time, you know what the film can and cannot do, and you have another proven facet to add to your photographic versatility.

If you are developing your own film, take the manufacturer's experience and knowledge at face value, for the beginning at least, and follow his recommended developing suggestions. Do not experiment with film-developer combinations until you have thoroughly tested and obtained satisfactory results with the suggested combinations. If you send your film to one of the professional processors, remember they are not mind readers. Give them and your film a fighting chance—tell them the ASA number you used to expose the film. It gives them a good starting point, even for developing by inspection.

Always use the same ASA number for an entire roll of film. For example, if you have doubled the rating, stick to it; do not go back to the normal rating halfway through the roll.

Film is inexpensive, the most inexpensive part of photography. Use it generously but not wastefully. Take enough shots so you are protected and have a very good chance of getting at least one fine shot per roll. If possible, bracket your shots as an insurance measure.

For shooting once-in-a-lifetime events, use cartridges or rolls of film with the larger number of shots. Time wasted reloading, in the middle of a wedding, for example, is lost, for once the moment has passed, it is gone. There is no second chance. Try to

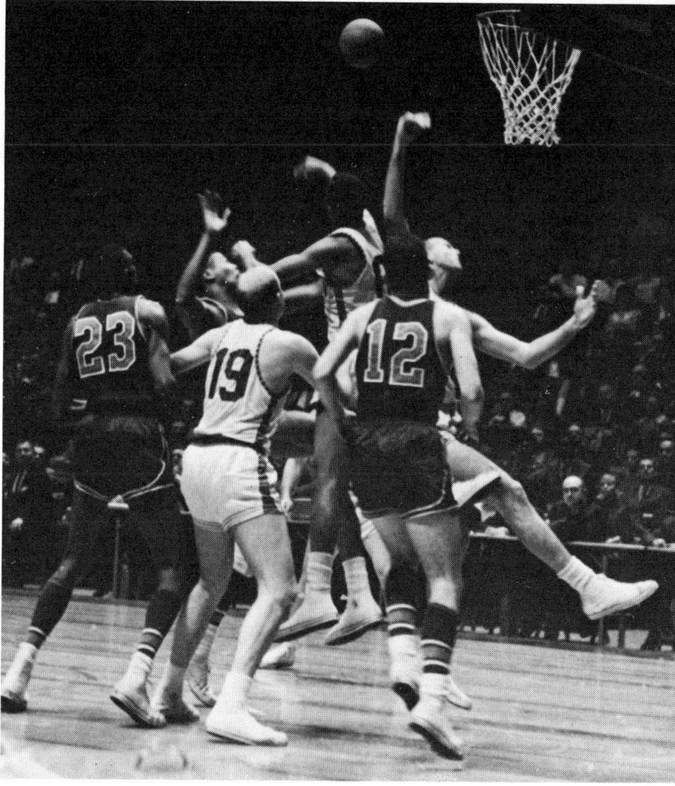

Plus-X film exposed at four times recommended ASA rating under available light conditions. DXF.

anticipate and schedule your shots beforehand, so you know approximately how many shots you will take of each situation. This will allow you to reload during a lull. Above all, make sure you carry enough film. It is better to take home two or three unopened rolls of film than to get stuck in the middle of the event, out of film, and with no place to buy it. Besides, if you carry more film, the chances are you will use it, thereby giving greater variety, greater selection, and greater opportunity to get terrific pictures.

The following charts of most popular films, available in a variety of sizes, will tell you at a glance which films are best suited to your purpose. Select several, then, after testing and by a systematic process of elimination, choose the one best suited to your particular photographic situation.

Film		Film Speed Daylight
SLOW	Adox KB 14	20
	Adox KB 17	40
	Adox KB 21	100
	Agfapan 100	100
	H & W Control VTE Pan	80
	Ilford Pan F	50
	Kodak Panatomic-X	32
MEDIUM	Fuji Neopan SSS	200
	GAF 125 Black-and-White Film	125
	Ilford FP4	125
	Kodak Plus-X Pan	125
	Kodak Verichrome Pan	125
FAST	Ilford HP4	400
	Kodak Recording Film Type 2475	1000-3200
	Kodak Royal-X Pan (roll)	1250
	Kodak Tri-X Pan	400
	Polaroid	
	Type 55 P/N	50
	Type 105	100
	Type 107	3000

COLOR FILMS (SLIDE OR TRANSPARENCY)

Film	Film Speed	
	Daylight	Tungsten
Agfachrome 64	64	20
Fujichrome R-100	100	80
GAF 64 Color Slide Film	64	16
GAF 200 Color Slide Film	200	100
GAF 500 Color Slide Film	500	250
Kodak Ektachrome Infrared Aero	100	—
Kodak Ektachrome-X	64	25
Kodak High Speed Ektachrome	160	50
Kodak High Speed Ektachrome Tungsten	80	125
Kodachrome 25	25	12
Kodachrome 64	64	25
Kodachrome II, Professional Type A	25	40
Sakura R100	100	32
3M Color Slide Film	50	16

COLOR FILMS, NEGATIVE

Film	Film Speed Daylight
Agfacolor CNS Color Print Film	80
Fujicolor N-100	100
GAF Color Print Film	80
Kodacolor II	80
Kodak Ektacolor Professional Type S	100
Kodak Vericolor II Professional Type S	100
Sakuracolor	80
3M Color Print Film	80

4

EXPOSE RIGHT FOR EVERY LIGHT

The key to better photography is better lighting, or more accurately, better use of lighting, in order to get the desired effects that are an integral and important part of better photographs. When used correctly, light can help a photographer produce any of a thousand different moods and feelings: glamour, eeriness, brightness, unhappiness, joy, sorrow, plenty, and poverty, to name but a few.

Despite its value as a basic element of photography, many amateur photographers simply regard light as a necessary, unpredictable evil. However, attention to the details of light and its properties (sunlight, artificial light, and special lighting conditions) should serve as a fine start toward better photographs.

SUNLIGHT

Outdoor photography, using sunlight as the primary source of illumination, offers the photographer just about the best source of light, but the one over which he has least control. With the exception of fill-in flash, reflectors, shading, and careful selection of time of day, the photographer can exercise little control over the actual light source, *but* he can make the most of what he has to get the kind of photos he wants. To do this, he can do several things in his own behalf. Since he cannot move his light source, he may move the subject to a selected spot, he may move his camera so it can make the most of the available light and shadows, he may use fill-in flash to eliminate some shadows, and he may use reflectors to soften other shadows, as well as planning his shooting for a certain time of day in order to take advantage of specific light and shadow conditions.

By moving either the camera or subject into position in relation to the source of sunlight, the photographer can take advantage of four basic lighting set-ups—front lighting, 45° sidelighting, 90° sidelighting, and backlighting.

For general use with both color and black-and-white film, 45° sidelighting is the best. With the sun supplying light at a 45° angle to the position of the camera, the subject can be most favorably photographed, without the deep, intrusive shadows of 90° sidelight or backlighting. The 45° sidelighting method should be used for most subjects where a pleasing, relatively soft quality is desired.

Front lighting, though producing a flat, almost toneless rendition on black-and-white film, is almost ideal for photos on color film, especially with simple cameras. Extremely safe as far as exposure is concerned, since the entire subject has the same overall light quality, the almost completely shadowless portrayal of the subject is boring and lacking in any third-dimensional effect or interest. However, since color film registers tonal differences in color, rather than in shades of gray, the front-lighting method is fine for color film. To insure even better photography using front lighting with color film, make sure the sun, which should be in back of the camera, is high, but not directly overhead, since this would cause deep color shadows, for example, in portraits, under eyes and nose.

To obtain reasonably strong dramatic effects, where harsh, deep shadows are an asset, 90° sidelighting will do the job. It is especially good for stark scenes, or for extremely masculine-looking male portraits, but 90° sidelighting can also be used for other purposes if a bright reflector is used to help soften the very strong shadows.

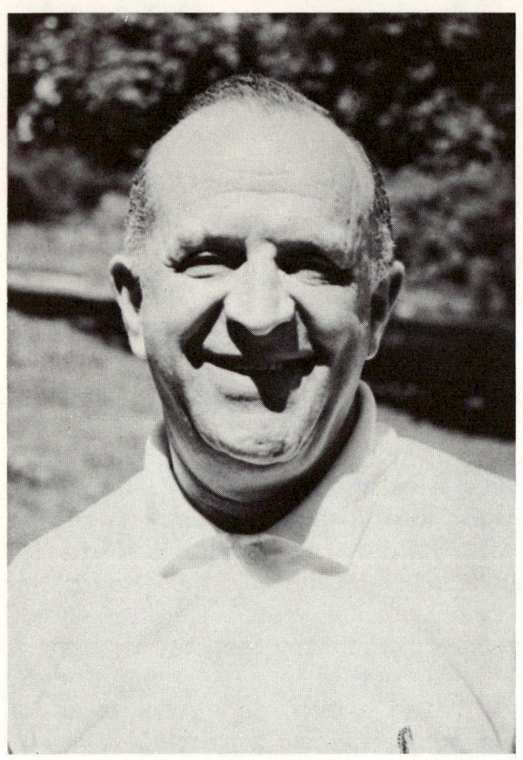

Sunlight almost directly overhead causes deep shadows under nose and eyes. DXF.

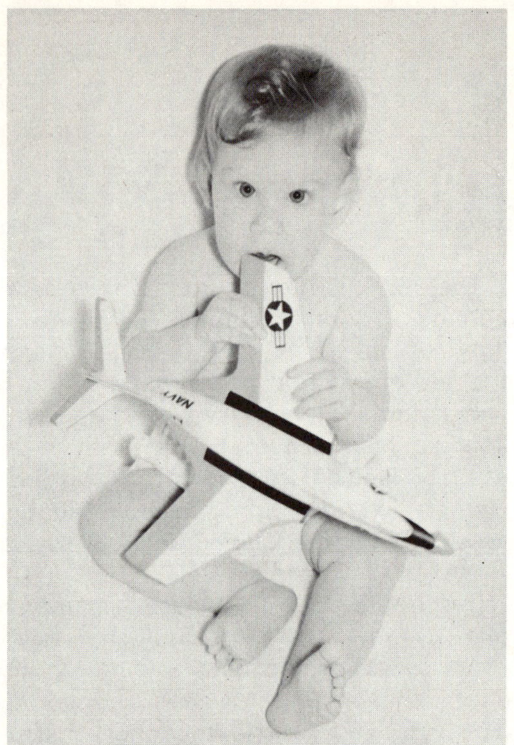

Flat, uninteresting front lighting eliminates much of the character that would liven this photo.

Silhouettes, which are highly dramatic and should therefore be used only for very special purposes, can be obtained by lighting from directly in back of the subject. When backlighting for the silhouette effect, be sure to protect your lens with a lens shade, for stray beams of light or glare may enter the lens and streak your film.

While on the subject of sunlight and the uses of outdoor light for photographic effects, correct exposure as well as several special cases should be mentioned. Normally, for photos with fine detail and little shadow problem, you take an exposure-meter reading from the subject, relate this to film speed, shutter speed, and desirable depth of field, directly on the exposure meter, and shoot your photo at correct settings. This is not always possible when shooting outdoors. When using sidelighting, usually over 45°, and backlighting, a meter reading of the general subject will not give sufficient information for a clear picture. Generally, in these cases, shadow areas are oppressively dark and heavy. To

avoid this, you can fill in some of the shadows before shooting with flash or reflectors, or you can vary your meter reading to consider the shadow areas. After taking careful close-up readings of both highlighted and deeply shadowed areas, equate the difference, arrive at a compromise setting, and shoot at this reading. Since most modern films have wide latitude, you will be sure of fine photos if you use this compromise meter-reading system for deeply shadowed areas.

On brightly reflecting areas, such as snow-covered land or beach sand, take the reflection into consideration and reduce your exposure. The reverse of course is true, when shooting naturally dark areas with very little light reflectance. As will be explained in Chapter 7, accessories such as filters, polarizers, and of course, flash and strobe units can be used to help you get other effects when shooting by sunlight. Remember, when you have a filter over the lens, apply the correct filter factor or your photos most surely will be underexposed.

32

ARTIFICIAL LIGHT

In addition to sunlight as a source of light for taking pictures, the amateur photographer can call on photofloods, flashbulbs, flash cubes, and electronic flash units, as well as available light. How he uses this variety of lighting methods, singly or mixed, is up to the whim or personal experience of each photographer. However he uses the various artificial lighting methods, he should first consider the conditions under which each operates and the conditions under which he expects to work. Once these are determined, several different combinations can be used with the assurance that the method has been thoroughly tested and can almost guarantee success.

Most floodlight photography is of the portrait variety, either portraits of people or portraits of things. For this facet of photography a classic lighting pattern has been perfected, derived from the lighting arrangements of many painters. A single key

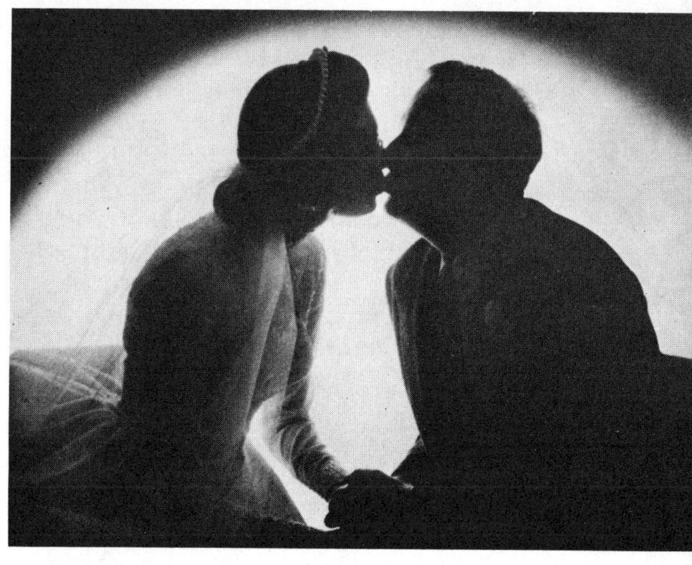

Silhouetting can be effective for special photos and occasions.

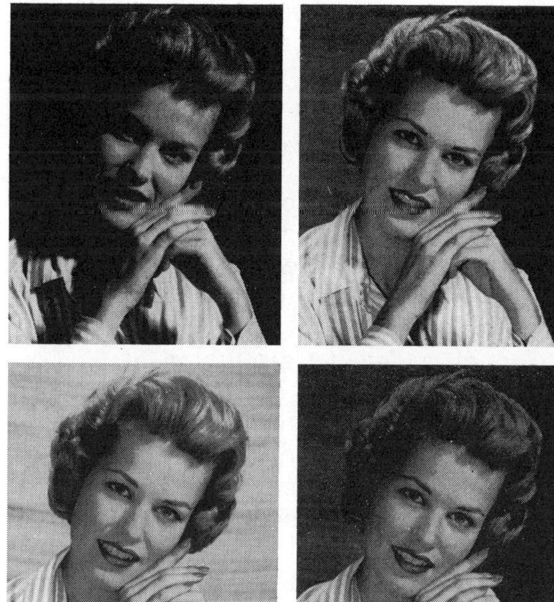

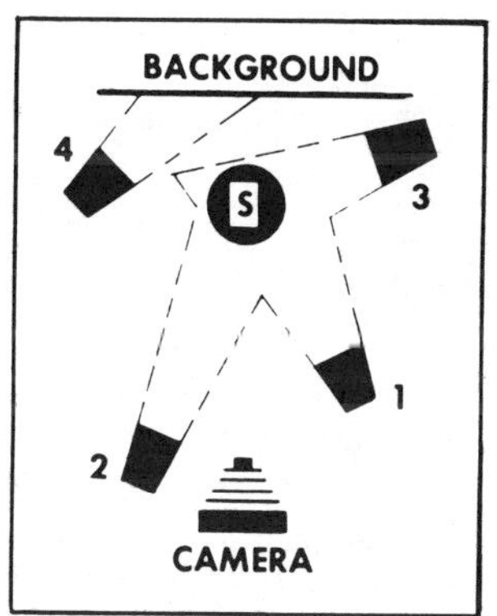

45° key light (1), plus fill light, low near camera (2), plus hair light (3), plus background light (4) result in a well-lighted photo (l to r). Photo courtesy of DuPont.

light is placed 45° from the camera lens axis; a more diffused light to lighten some of the shadows cast by the key light, and optionally, other lights are added to light the background and supply highlighting to specific parts of the subject. Though this lighting arrangement will just about guarantee a beautifully exposed photo, other effects suitable to the specific situation should be tried, experimentation showing the best lighting for each shooting session.

For better photographs using photofloods, do not try to eliminate all shadows from the subject. Eliminating shadows eliminates character, leaving the face flat and unattractive. Instead of doing away with all shadows, move the lights around so the shadows fall where you want them to, highlighting good features and playing down poor ones. If you have worked out a lighting arrangement you like, and it has proved to be good for your situation, sketch a quick diagram of this set-up and file it for future reference. Since photoflood lights can be hot and uncomfortable for the subject, speed and efficiency in equipment use is important. Compact, completely cordless units such as are usually used for movies are excellent and readily adaptable to still photography.

Bounce lighting has become one of the best methods to light a subject fully without having him squint and stare uncomfortably into a battery of floodlights. As a matter of fact, since bounce lighting, which consists of using lamps with reflectors aimed at the ceiling or other white reflecting surface, is softer and less critical than direct lighting, a good arrangement can be left standing and used for almost all similar or nearly similar situations.

To gain good modeling as well as great flexibility through bounce lighting, use more than one lamp in your lighting set-up. Place one lamp near the subject, aimed at the ceiling, and a second unit on one side,

reflecting off the wall and filling in many shadows. The first light will give an excellent, well-defined light and dark shadow pattern, a bit softer than that obtained with a normal 45° lighting arrangement. The second unit will fill in the dark shadow areas, supplying enough light to highlight facial characteristics and put catch lights in the eyes.

Background lighting is merely the use of one diffused lamp positioned close enough to the background to wash out any of the shadows cast by the subject and generally raise the tone level. Since backgrounds are best left simple, it is usually a fine idea to pose a subject before a completely blank light-colored wall, and then wash out any undesirable shadows. To add a bit of variety to your background lighting, use a gimmick used by many advertising studios as well as movie and television technicians—a light pattern. Project the pattern on a blank wall behind the subject by sending light through a cardboard cutout known as a "cookie." Naturally, there are few limits to the size and patterns available for use in this manner. Just don't overdo a good thing and have the background pattern more interesting and important than the subject.

To adjust the contrast of this background pattern, adjust the amount of light thrown by both the background light and the light behind the cardboard cutout. To soften the pattern on the wall behind the subject, adjust the distance between the light and the pattern as well as the distance between the pattern and the wall.

Though a detailed discussion of flashguns and strobe lights could easily fall into this chapter, it has been placed in the chapter on accessories. Therefore, no further discussion is warranted at this point. Instead, a discussion of exposures and exposure techniques should show how to get the very best from any and all lighting situations.

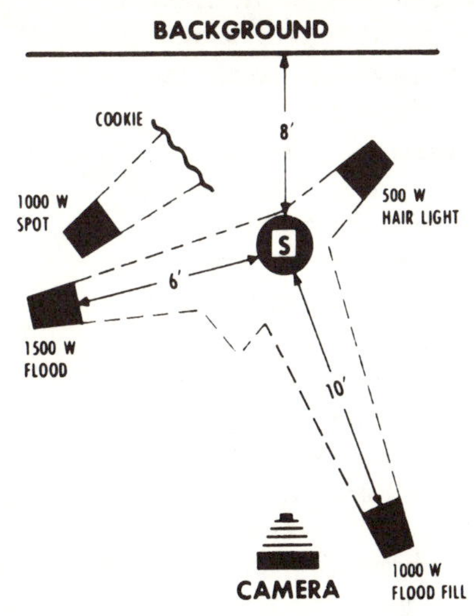

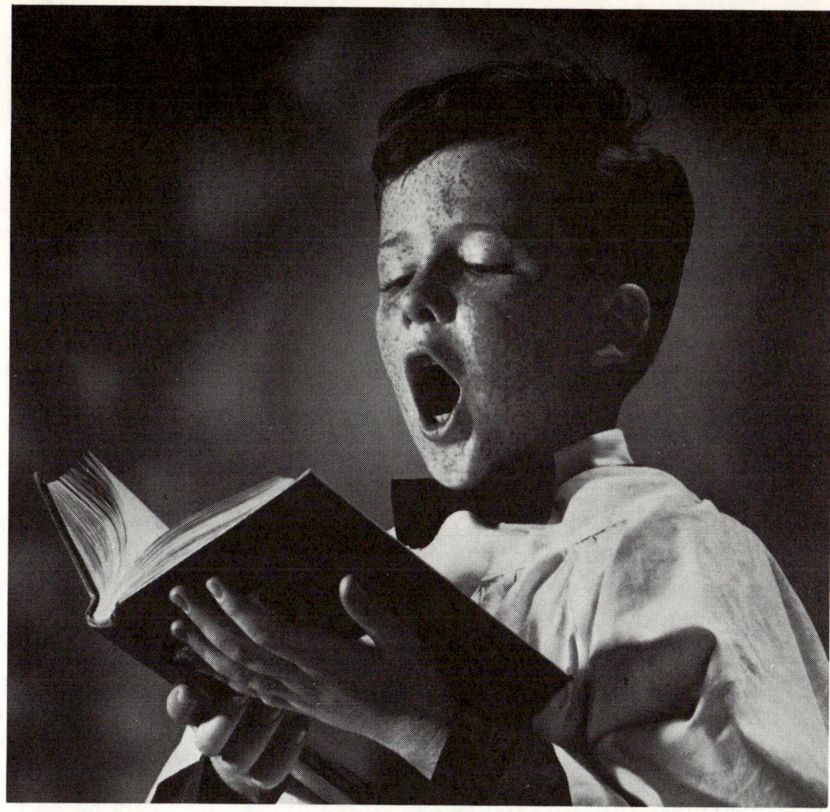

Well-lit subject with soft, interesting background produced by use of cardboard "cookie." Photo courtesy of DuPont.

EXPOSURE

Despite the exposure latitude built into most films, a considerable amount of control must be exercised to obtain a good negative. The idea is to expose correctly and get the good negative in this way, rather than to rely upon film latitude.

To get an acceptably good negative, exposure must take all variables into consideration and equate them so the resultant negative gives fine detail in the areas of deepest shadow as well as the areas of brightest highlight, and of course all the areas in between. For most amateurs, it is extremely fortunate there is more than one "right combination" to produce a good negative.

Two basic factors give the proper exposure for the subject, and these two factors must be closely interrelated to be of any use to the photographer—the film speed and the subject brightness. Once determined, these factors are used as starting points for the addition of other information, such as shutter speed, and calculations that establish lens aperture, or the other way around. The selection of film with a good range of tonal qualities will greatly enhance your chances of obtaining a good, solid negative, neither too hard nor too soft. However, also take advantage of those films which have shorter tonal ranges, and as a result, give darker shadow areas and lighter white areas.

To find out the brightness of the subject, an exposure meter is the best bet, since objects are difficult to estimate visually for brightness. Professionals, relying on many years of experience in similar situations, can get an accurate visual estimate of subject brightness, but the amateur should rely on the more accurate eye of an exposure meter.

Meters are not necessary, and most would be useless for lighting by flash or strobe units. By simply working out an elementary arithmetic problem centered around lamp-to-subject distance and film speed, as well as a guide number supplied with the bulbs, an extremely accurate exposure can be found. Similar guide numbers can be applied to certain photoflood lamps with built-in reflectors, and in these cases should be used after extremely accurate measurement of lamp-to-subject distance. With the photofloods, small distance errors can make great differences in exposure.

For better photographs, mastery of the exposure meter as well as a working knowledge of film quality and properties are important. To these should be added several suggestions you may already know, but which bear repeating for those who have heard them before and need mentioning for those who have not.

When working out the settings for a particular photographic situation, always try to end up with a lens opening somewhere away from the two ends of the scale. Many problems can come up at either end of the lens opening scale, and since nothing, or very little, can be gained by a bigger or smaller opening, stay away from the extremes whenever possible.

In cases where there is little you can do about the contrast, or lack of contrast, of a subject, expose for whatever contrast there is, and avoid flat lighting. Flat lighting tends to remove all character except, as mentioned, with color film.

If you can do something to add or remove shadows, place them where they will do the most good to accentuate important points and features. Remember to measure both the highlighted areas and the shadow areas and then arrive at a compromise exposure setting.

Whatever the exposure setting or film used, be certain it is right for the situation. Carefully thought out and executed shooting sessions, considering all the advantages and disadvantages present, coupled with extreme care in film selection and exposure, cannot help but give you better photos. All of photography requires careful attention to details, but it is the attention to lighting and exposure that pays off most in better pictures.

5

AN IMPORTANT INGREDIENT...
THE SUBJECT

With the preceding information and suggestions about cameras, film, exposures, and lighting, it should be possible to take fine photos. However, something is missing. Though many amateurs take it for granted, preferring to concentrate on technical excellence for photo improvement, lack of a good subject can make the best-looking photo only so-so. What good is a sharp, carefully lighted, correctly exposed, precisely developed, and meticulously printed photo, if the subject is nondescript or lost in a maze of confusing background or props? A well-composed subject, therefore, is the key to an eye-catching photograph.

COMPOSITION

Before any discussion of proper subject and subject treatment can get under way, the important field of photographic composition must be explored. What is it that makes many amateurs feel composition consists of equal parts of luck, chance, and wishing? Accepting their photographic fate from the will of the gods, these amateurs go along, blindly snapping photos of anything and everything unfortunate enough to pass before their lenses. When shown beautifully composed and executed photographs, they scoff and say, "He certainly is a lucky photographer." For those who would rather depend on talent, experience, and knowledge rather than luck to get fine photos, the rules of composition will aid immeasurably. Putting these rules to use, instead of scoffing, will help photographers get better pictures.

1. Tell a story. Tell a single story. Though the subject can be more than a single object, make sure it is not a jumble of unrelated things, bound only by the picture frame, telling nothing. The subject should dominate, telling the viewer almost all he wants to know about the picture.

2. Do not use a single, bare element in a photo unless it is a record shot or portrait. Small, subdued elements help complete the picture and tell the viewer the remainder of the story.

3. Check the background; don't make it too outstanding or allow it to dominate the principal subject. Look all around the subject area to make sure no foreign objects or foolish effects will appear in the picture (such as a tree behind the subject that, in the finished picture, will appear to be growing out of the subject's head).

4. Have everything in tune—background, subject, and supporting elements. All parts of the photo must go together. Dissimilar objects are confusing and do little for the photo.

5. Use shadows and light patterns to advantage in highlighting the subject. Used correctly, shadows can point up a main interest area. Used incorrectly, they can pull the eye away from the subject or main interest point, becoming the subject themselves.

6. Place the center of interest off-center in the frame. Exact centering is dull, annoying to the eye, and often will not attract sufficient attention.

7. Divide your picture area into uneven sections. As mentioned above, interest can be lost if all areas are equal.

8. Balance a picture, but do not make it symmetrical. Elements should help complete a photo, and lead the viewer's eye to the main area.

9. Lights and darks should be balanced within a picture. Do not put all light or dark areas in a single area—divide them up to balance and add interest to the photo.

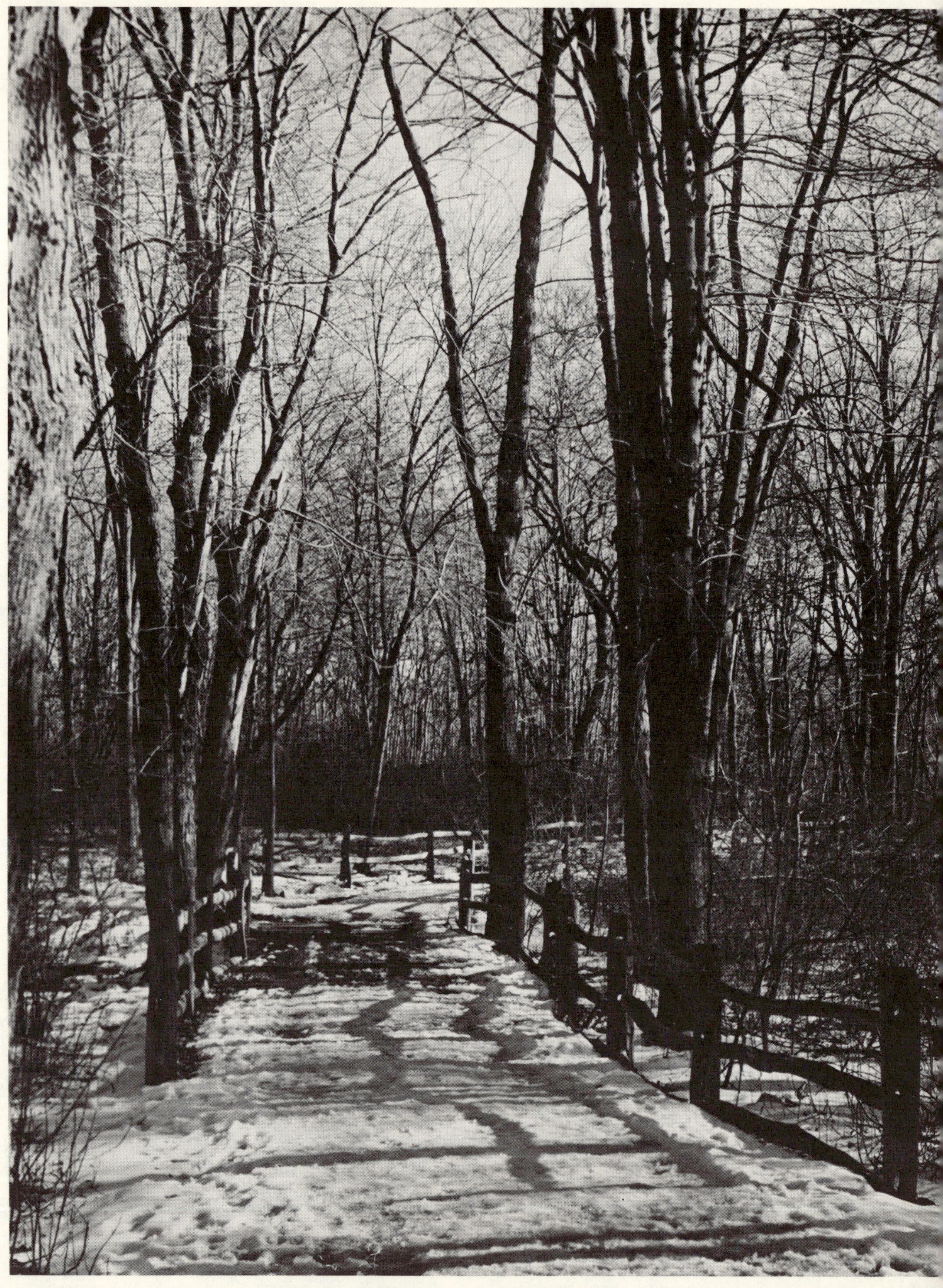

10. Use figures in landscape scenes or photos of natural phenomena to give a feeling of size. Make sure the person stands at least 25 to 30 feet from the camera, and to one side.

11. Use interesting lines as a device to draw attention to a subject or special feature of a photo. If the lines intersect at close to a right angle, the eye will quickly be drawn to the meeting point.

12. Lines that run out of a picture will pull the eye along with them, and the viewer's gaze will move away from the picture.

13. Do not allow a line to cut your photo in half, as would, for example, a horizontal line through the center of the photo.

14. Use a natural arrangement within your photos. Arrange objects in the photo so the eye will move in a natural, logical sequence from one to the next. Keep the viewer's eye from being confused.

15. Retain only those parts of the photo that are necessary and add something to the photo. A too large expanse of sky, foreground, or background rarely does anything to contribute to the value of the photo.

16. Select camera angles that do the most for the subject. Most things will be more attractive and more interesting when photographed at an angle, rather than head-on.

17. Don't jam too many people into the middle of a photo. This looks like a mob scene on the corner waiting for a bus. People in a photo (as well as waiting for a bus) need "air" space around them.

18. Small, light spots on a dark background attract attention more readily than dark spots on a light background. Remember this, and if possible, use it to your advantage.

19. Mix light and dark areas together so these elements don't "fight for promin-

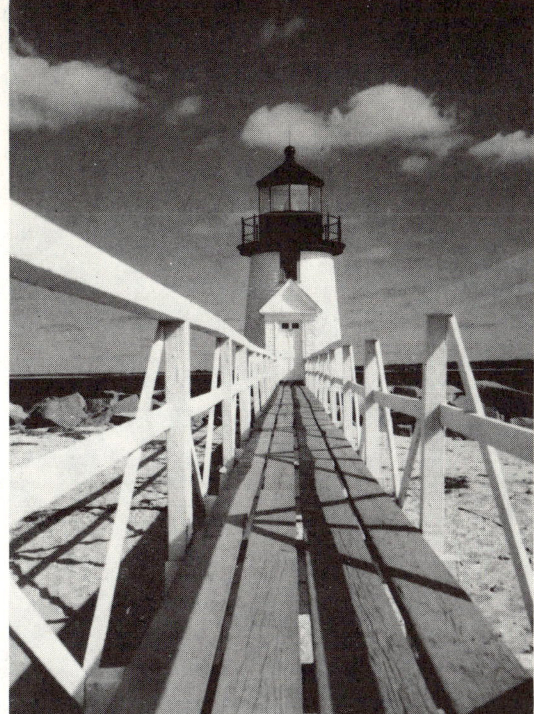

"Nantucket," shot with a Polaroid Land camera, illustrates how lines may be used to good advantage. Photo by Lee Mooney.

ence," distracting the eye from the center of interest.

20. When people are photographed along with landscapes or scenery, have them look at the scene rather than straight into the camera. This gives the impression of a candid shot, one taken while the person was actually looking at this sight.

21. For special lighting and shadow effects, schedule your shooting for specific times of the day. Anticipating shadows and where and how they are going to fall, you can easily include them in your picture, safe in the knowledge they will be where you want them.

22. Try to have the viewer's eye enter the picture from the lower left-hand side. This is a natural entrance point, and makes the photo seem more natural.

23. Parallel lines can wreak havoc upon a picture. They are distracting, and can cause the photo to have dual interest points vying for predominance.

Every photo has a viewpoint. We follow this fence around the curve and off to somewhere. Photo by Linda Page.

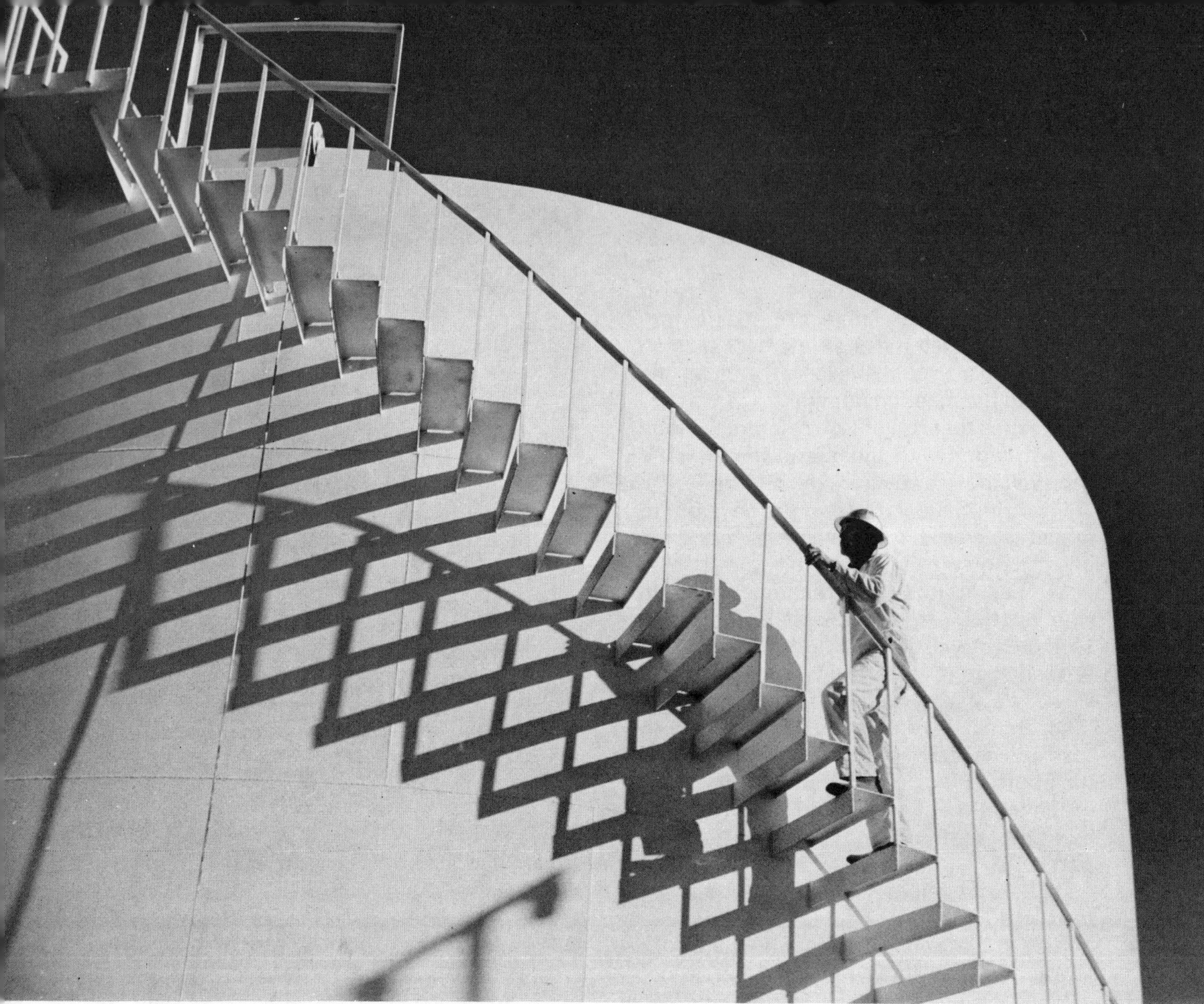

Effective use of light and shadow made "Industry" a prizewinner. Photo by Danny Poush.

24. The outer edges of your photo area are a part of the total picture effect. The shapes that appear at these edges should be varied and interesting but always subordinate.

25. To check for good composition, turn the photo upside-down. If it still seems nice, balanced, and interesting, pat yourself on the back; your photo is truly well composed.

26. Use your own taste, good sense, and personal preference to determine good composition. If you can honestly say your photo is pleasant to look at, uncomplicated, and simply arranged to make viewing easy, then your composition, and most likely your photo as well, is better than average. Develop this sense of composition so it becomes natural for you to have well-composed photos. Well-composed photos are better photos.

All photographic rules, about composition or anything else, concern themselves in the final analysis with the proper presentation of a subject. Since better than one-third of all amateur photos are taken of children, this subject area deserves a considerable amount of careful study.

CHILDREN

To get better photos of children, get them on your side, for once on your side, most children will happily participate in your picture-taking adventures as if they were some sort of wonderful game. The reverse, unfortunately, is also true. Annoy a child, make a big production out of every snapshot, and you are a sure bet to get nothing more than a deeply implanted dislike of cameras, photos, and photographers.

The miracle of birth starts many people thinking about, among other things, photography. Few proud papas are willing to let any of the magnificent first moments of their children's lives pass unphotographed. Fine pictures can be taken at the hospital, despite many people's fears that hospitals do not allow picture-taking. This is not true for the most part, unless you make yourself unwelcome by overdoing a good thing. For these, and most other photos of infants and toddlers, as well as those of older children, color film should be used as often as possible. High Speed Ektachrome and GAF 200 and 500 Color Slide films will permit available light photos, while the other color films are fine when used in conjunction with flashbulbs or strobe units. Another misconception, that of flashbulbs being bad for an infant's eyes, has been disproved. However, if you do not wish to use them, or if perhaps the individual hospital disapproves, available light is most satisfactory. When using flashbulbs or electronic flash units aimed into the glass windows of the nursery, stand at a 45° angle to the window to eliminate flashback from the light unit.

Once home, the picture-taking possibilities with babies are unlimited. A fine idea, which reaps higher and higher dividends as the child grows older, is a chronological record of the many "firsts" during a baby's initial year. To help keep this record in correct order, slip a lettered strip, telling the baby's age, into the picture.

At the beginning, with the baby doing little besides eating and sleeping, the photographer can take his time and shoot with infinite care and deliberation. This will change as the baby grows older. For the best shots of any children, no matter what their ages, keep them within their own environment and with their own toys and possessions. Do not try to make them look older than they are, and don't rush them. They will do everything in due time—crawl, sit, stand, walk—and you will be able to picture them doing all these things when the proper time comes. Remember, this is a record of what they are doing as well as when they are doing it. No cheating.

As the child gets older, the shutter speed you use must increase. Whether you use flash, available light, or whatever, this should make no difference to the child. Picture-taking should not be terribly special, but rather an almost everyday thing, like a game. Keep a child at ease, and your pictures will be wonderful. Force a child and you are not only wasting film, but may also be creating a problem you may never solve.

Once on your side, children go about their business becoming natural, fine subjects. DXF.

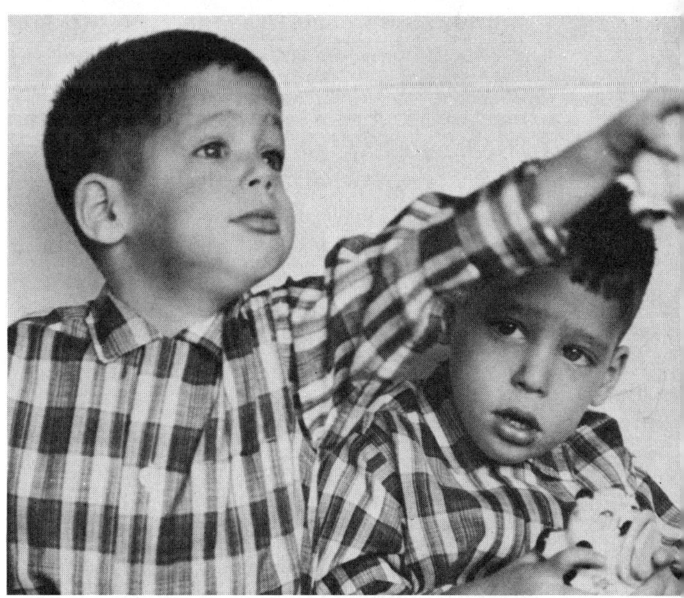

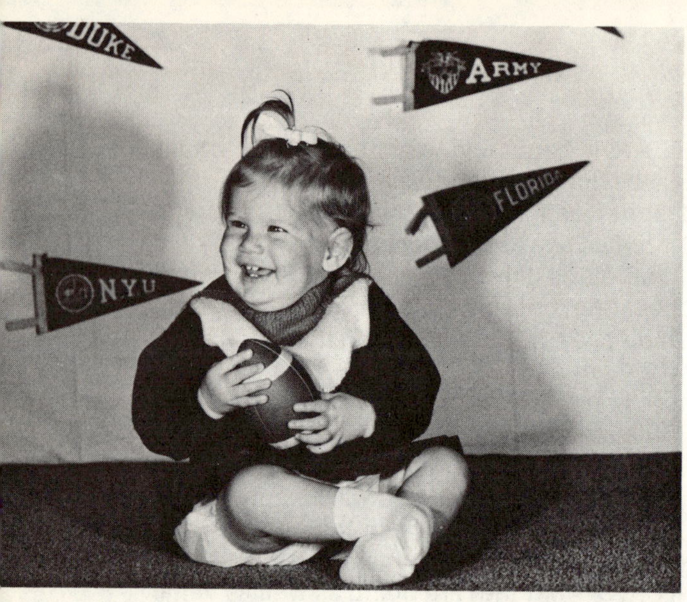

A child enjoying the "photography game," plenty of film, and some patience help you get good baby photos. DXF.

For better shots of children of all ages:

1. Have them "help you" take the pictures. Their partnership is invaluable in retaining their interest and cooperation.

2. Keep them in their own environment, doing the things that are natural for them to do. Stiffly posed pictures, no matter how good, are seldom as good as one unposed, candid shot.

3. Make use of natural surroundings—bathtub, high chair, playpen, crib—to add the variety and interest in every child's life.

4. Be thoroughly prepared long before you are going to take a picture. Children lose interest and patience quickly, so don't fumble. Know what you want, and get it.

5. Try as many "child in motion" pictures as possible, since these tell the story later on.

6. If the child has a pet, use it in pictures with the child. They are "naturals" together.

7. Take as many pictures as you possibly can, without making a nuisance of yourself and getting the child angry or annoyed.

8. Keep many albums of your children, as suggested in Chapter 11, not only of firsts, but of the things that best represent the individual character of your children.

9. Take only those pictures that are in good taste and will not embarrass the youngster later in life. If you must take the "bare bottom" type shot, keep it in a separate file.

10. Enjoy your children and your photographing of them. The joy and general delight will radiate from the photos and slides.

TEEN-AGERS

With babies and children it is a good idea to take many photographs candidly, unobserved. It is a must when photographing teen-agers. At this in-between age, the subjects are not only unwilling to be photographed, but often find another place to be whenever a camera appears.

For better photos of teen-agers, take advantage of the many deep interests in the teen-ager's life. While on the phone, getting ready for a date, immersed in records, installing lug nuts on a hot rod, and consuming unbelievable quantities of food, most teen-agers are wonderfully comfortable and will most likely be oblivious to your picture-taking. Not only can you get your picture, but you will get the teen-agers the way they are, at ease, happy, and doing what they like to do.

It is true photographers should always strive to make their subjects look as good as possible, but nowhere is it as important as with the awkward-age teen-agers. Skin problems, facial characteristics, and general awkwardness should be played down by diffused lighting, careful angle selection, and where necessary, retouching. Retouching should always be a last-chance remedy. Try everything possible before shooting, to eliminate any area that might lead to awkward or self-conscious points having to be retouched. Highlight the good points, subdue the poor ones, and your subject might even start posing willingly, after seeing how good a few of your candid shots come out.

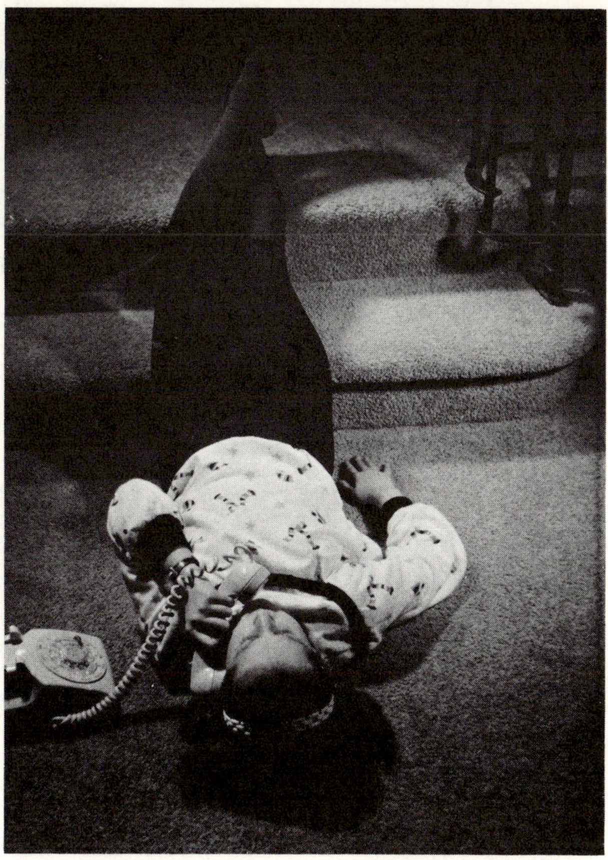

A teen-ager, posed or "caught" in a natural position, provides an interesting and interested subject. DXF.

ADULTS

Adults are just like children, only older. As a result, most of the suggestions for better photos of children apply to adults as well.

One of the first questions raised concerning photographing adults is, how? How should they be posed once they have been convinced this whole thing is necessary? The most obvious techniques for photographing adults are those of formal portraiture. This method allows the photographer to capture the true character of the subject. However, since fine portraiture requires a studio and the equipment that usually fills a studio, it might be a better idea to leave this field to the studio photographer and concentrate on improving your own candid photography.

For better photos of adults, catch them as they are, or if you are posing them, arrange them in a characteristic setting. The photo of a man or woman doing the things he or she likes best and does most often has a natural charm that will carry through to final print. If grandma is a garden putterer, or Aunt Betty is an aspiring writer, pose them in their natural environment, and you will have people at ease. People at ease look good. People who are at ease, and look good, will be happy to pose again.

When posing a person, make sure he is the most important part of the photo, and as central interest, does not have to combat other outstanding features. Backgrounds should be simple, and if not essential to the photo, can be blurred by using a short depth of field.

Props should be large enough to be definable and give the subject something comfortable to do with his hands, but should not be overpowering. Lighting should assure a smooth, flattering rendition of face and facial characteristics, especially with older subjects. Soft lighting, gained by using one light near the camera, and another to fill in shadows and highlights, is most useful. Special effects can be arranged by making the lighting a bit more stark, but be careful not to overdo it, or you will make your subject look eerie, not interesting. If you plan to use flash for these photos, try to have some of the shadowy areas filled in by additional light sources or reflecting materials. Do not plan to remove blemishes from finished prints by retouching. Often these marks are recognizable as part of the person's character. It is a better idea to play down blemishes of all sorts by subdued lighting on these areas and correct use of focusing angle.

The mention of retouching, especially as it relates to adults, brings an important caution to mind. Retouching is an aid, not a panacea. It will not cure all print ills. Too much retouching on a face tends to make it lose character as lines are removed. The face becomes pasty or putty-like, and totally lacking in character. Since lines and spots and bumps are what make a person a particular person, leave them alone. Retouching will remove that which is normally there, making a face with depth and personality look flat and unreal. To make your subject look as good as possible, take the precaution beforehand. That's what you are striving to do when you try to become a better photographer, not to fix your mistakes after it's too late.

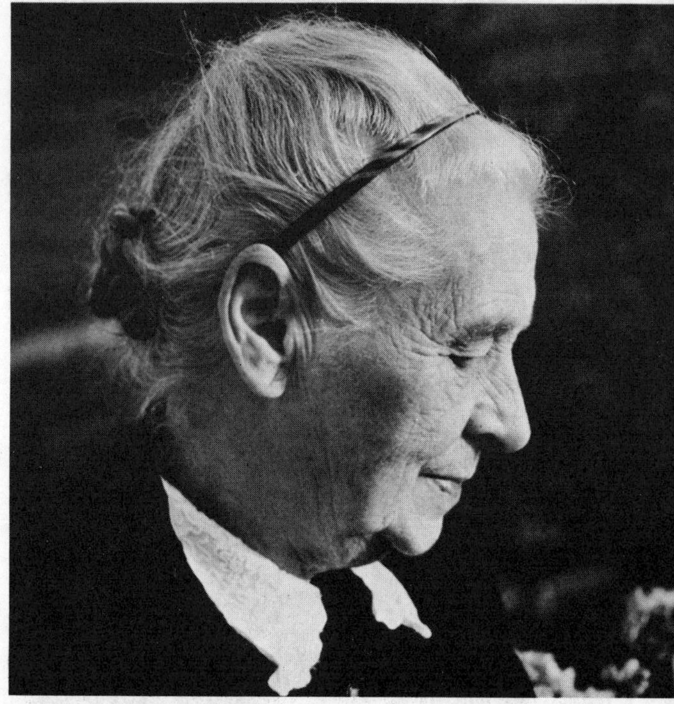

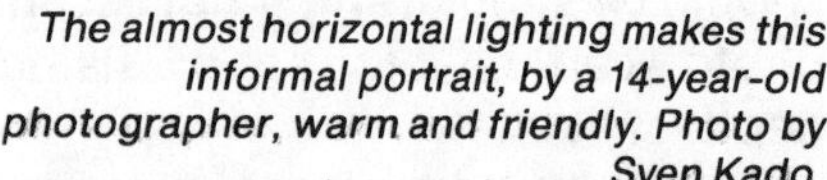
The almost horizontal lighting makes this informal portrait, by a 14-year-old photographer, warm and friendly. Photo by Sven Kado.

NATURE

Simplicity and ease of viewing should be the keywords for all photography, but especially for nature photography. Of course, color film gives a breathtaking picture even more depth and dimension, but many fine scenes can be captured with black-and-white films. Whatever the film you use for outdoor scenery, keep your shots simple, uncluttered, and make the most of what you see.

Unlike photography in which you control many or all of the elements, nature photography puts the picture before you, asking you to supply only the imagination and perception necessary to capture it on film. Rolling hills, glens, freshly plowed fields, farm houses, and the like, all offer scenic beauty to the photographer. In addition, any scene that means something special to you has four different faces, as supplied by the four seasons. Make the most of the stark, white mantle of winter, the gentle awakening of spring, the rich, full blooming of the hills during summer, and the magic palette of fall colors—from one scene.

You don't have to go deep into rural areas to find these wonders of nature. City dwellers can find a bit of the rolling countryside little more than a short auto ride away. Once found, nature photography enlists your aid and taste in recording. For better nature photography, apply everything your experience has taught you, and add a measure of photographic seeing. Compose in your mind's eye and then in the viewfinder. Select objects, scenes, and photo parts that fit together comfortably and complement each other, making your rural-type photography soft, quiet looking, and inviting.

Make the best possible use of natural lines, lights, and shadows. Tree limbs, cloud formations, water reflections, and other forms await you and your imagination. Filters, used correctly, can also be a great help in getting special effects and color renditions. Whatever might interest you can be found in nature or outdoor photography. It is up to the photographer to find it and then make the most of it.

44

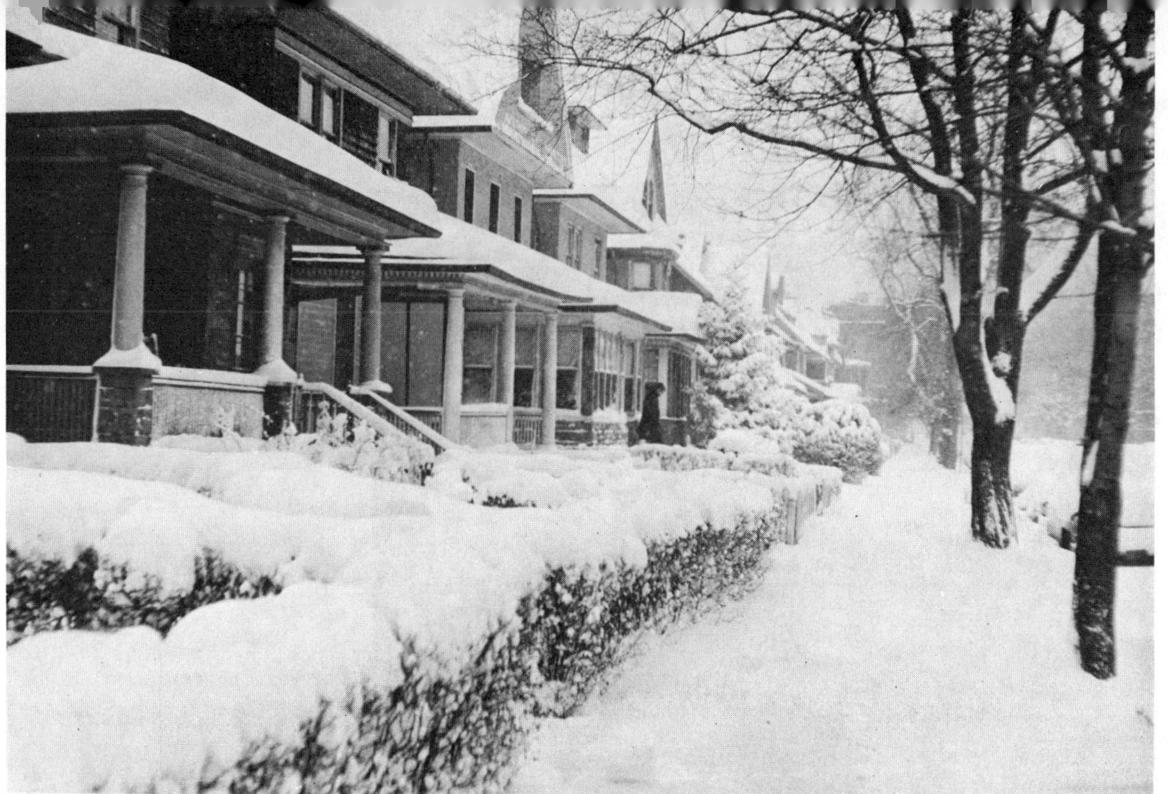

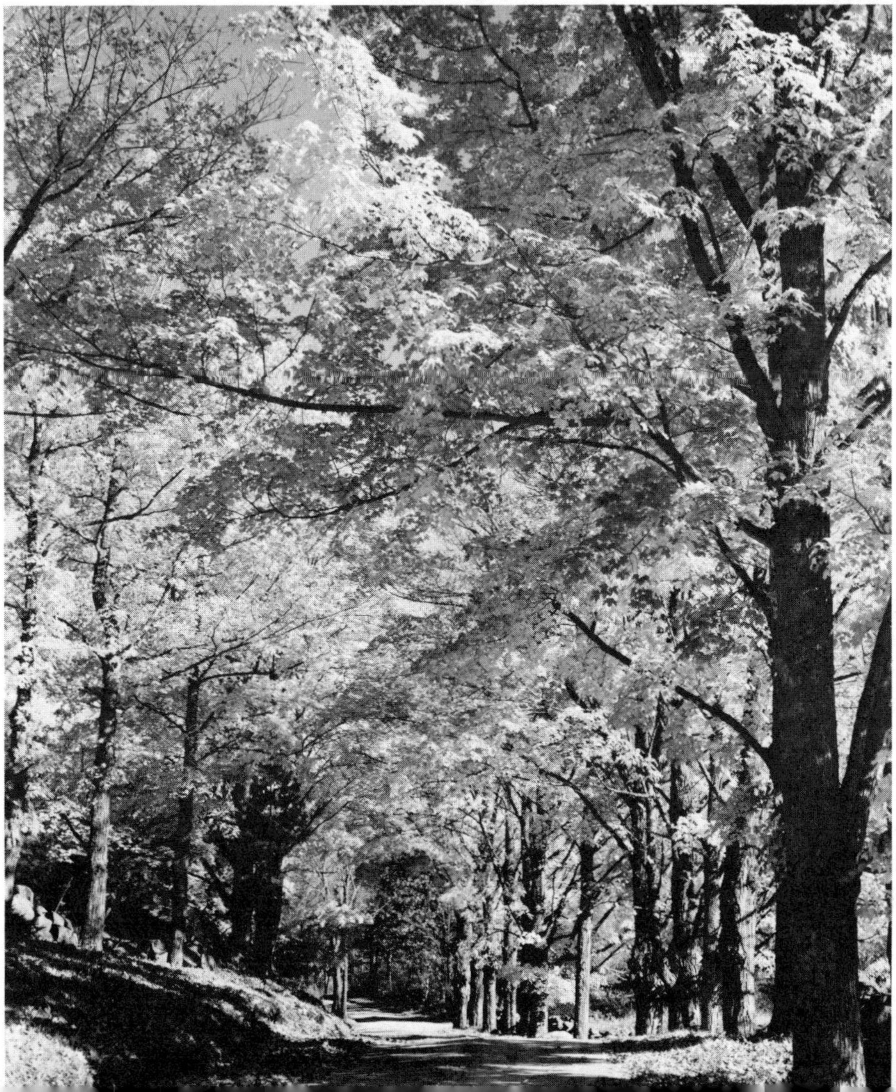

(Above) A commonplace scene, early on a winter morning, can make an effective picture. DXF. (Left) Tree-lined paths can be found anywhere; you only need to see them and make the most of them. Photo courtesy of GAF.

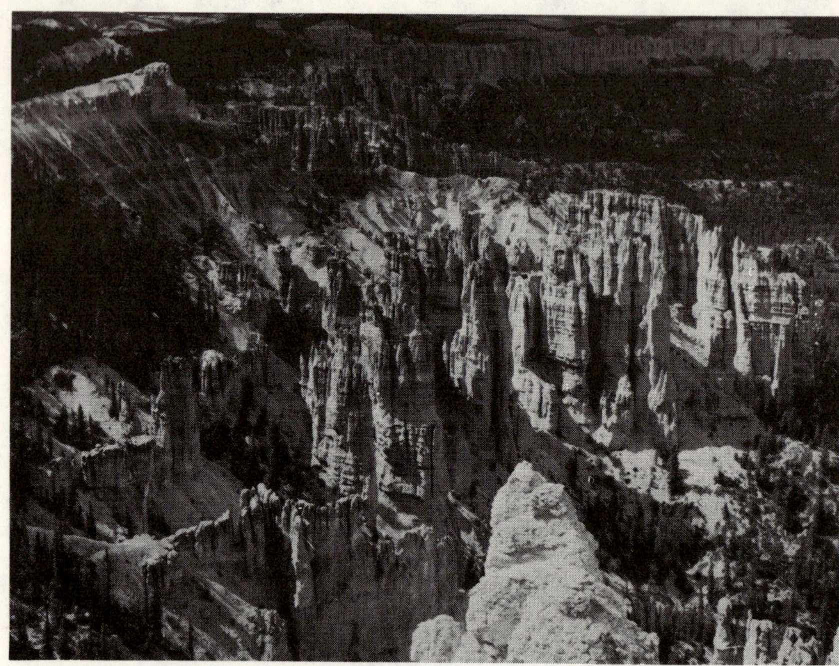

Bryce Canyon through the eyes of a teen-ager and the lens of a Rolleiflex. Photo by Simon Trutt.

SPECIAL OCCASIONS

Please . . . don't make a nuisance of yourself at special occasions: weddings, parties, and the like, by continually annoying the guests for one more shot, or blinding them with flashbulb after flashbulb. You will find that by blending into the group and taking unposed, candid shots, your photos will be more relaxed and natural. When you leave, you may have as many friends as you had when you got there, if not more.

At a party, a 35mm camera, or an ultra-miniature camera, is the most inconspicuous. Using a fast film allows you to do away with bulbs and get fine candid photos. With a Polaroid Land camera, you can even show the results of your candid work the same evening. Whatever your camera, make it a welcome guest by using it in good taste. Be careful, or not only may your cam-era be excluded from the next party, but you as well.

Weddings and other religious special occasions require careful preplanning. A full knowledge of the religion and its protocol is required. If professional photographers are in attendance, let them do the job they have been paid to do. Don't hinder them or get in their way. If you stick to candids and are not a nuisance, they will most likely treat you as an associate. Within a church or temple, your best bet is to remain as inconspicuous as possible. This is best done by using available light. Popping flashbulbs are annoying and do much to spoil the religious reverence of a ceremony.

Try to remember, special occasions call for candids, and candids call for available light whenever possible. This should enable you to record many fine affairs without spoiling the pleasure for you or the other guests.

6

IMPROVEMENT IS THE SPICE OF PHOTOGRAPHY

Certain errors plague almost all amateur photographers, ruining many photos and labeling the photographer as a beginner. Since the purpose of this chapter is to show some beautiful photos taken by amateurs, and thus give you the incentive to improve your own work, we shall note these very common errors, but not picture them. Surely all amateur photographers are familiar with these problems and would rather see fine pictures than those which illustrate errors, and which we have all seen far too many times in our own photos.

1. Double exposure—exposing two different photos on a single frame of film, unintentionally, is no way to economize. Get into the habit of advancing the film immediately after each exposure.

2. Obstructed lens—fingers, lens caps, camera-case straps, and other incidental equipment do not belong in front of the lens when you are shooting. A last-second check, prior to shooting, should prevent this from happening. Dirt on a lens also photographs beautifully, so check and clean the lens before shooting.

3. Subject surgery—heads and ears should not be chopped off by photographers. More care in using the viewfinder and correction for parallax will take care of this problem.

4. Leaning-tower photos—keep the camera level. A horizontal line within the photo will give you the correct camera angle orientation.

5. Blurred subject—either the camera was moved, or at the last minute the subject moved. To remedy the former, do not "snap" picture or shutter, press down gently; to remedy the latter, nail subject into position or use a faster shutter speed.

6. Out of focus—determine the true focus of the subject, not background, and carefully check just prior to shooting. This will avoid the problem of in-focus background and out-of-focus subject.

7. Bad background—interesting backgrounds are fine, but make sure they are not so interesting they become more important than the subject. Check also to see they do not distract because of color, form, etc., and that trees do not grow from people's heads.

8. Light flare—usually caused by a light leak somewhere within the camera. Don't try to fix it yourself; this is a job for a camera repairman. It can also be caused by reflected light bouncing back into the camera lens. Your best bets for curing these ills are having the lens shade on the camera at all times, and careful use of a polarizing filter.

9. Subject discomfort—the unhappy squint on your subject's face is directly proportional to his degree of discomfort. Do not put subject in position to look directly into sun. Let sun come over your shoulder at an angle, and let it fall, in that same or similar angle, on the subject. This makes for better lighting, better pictures, and happier subjects.

10. Underexposure—dark, heavy-looking photos, with little contrast between lights and darks, are the result of underexposure. Open up diaphragm, cut shutter speed, or

check and heed exposure-meter readings.

11. Overexposure—light, thin prints, with little feeling of reality, are caused by overexposure. The remedy is the opposite of underexposure—close the diaphragm, increase shutter speed, and similarly check and heed exposure-meter readings. Also helpful are record cards so aperture, shutter speed, etc., can be checked with results, corrected, and same mistakes not made again.

This list of most common amateur camera errors is, of course, incomplete. Each of us has his own favorite common camera error. Only experience and photo comparisons will remedy them. The photos that follow will prove amateur photographers can take fine photos, no matter what their age, experience, or the complexity of equipment they used. It should give you encouragement, ideas, and inspiration so you, too, can take better photographs.

Shimmering Lights. Photo by Frederick E. Annette.

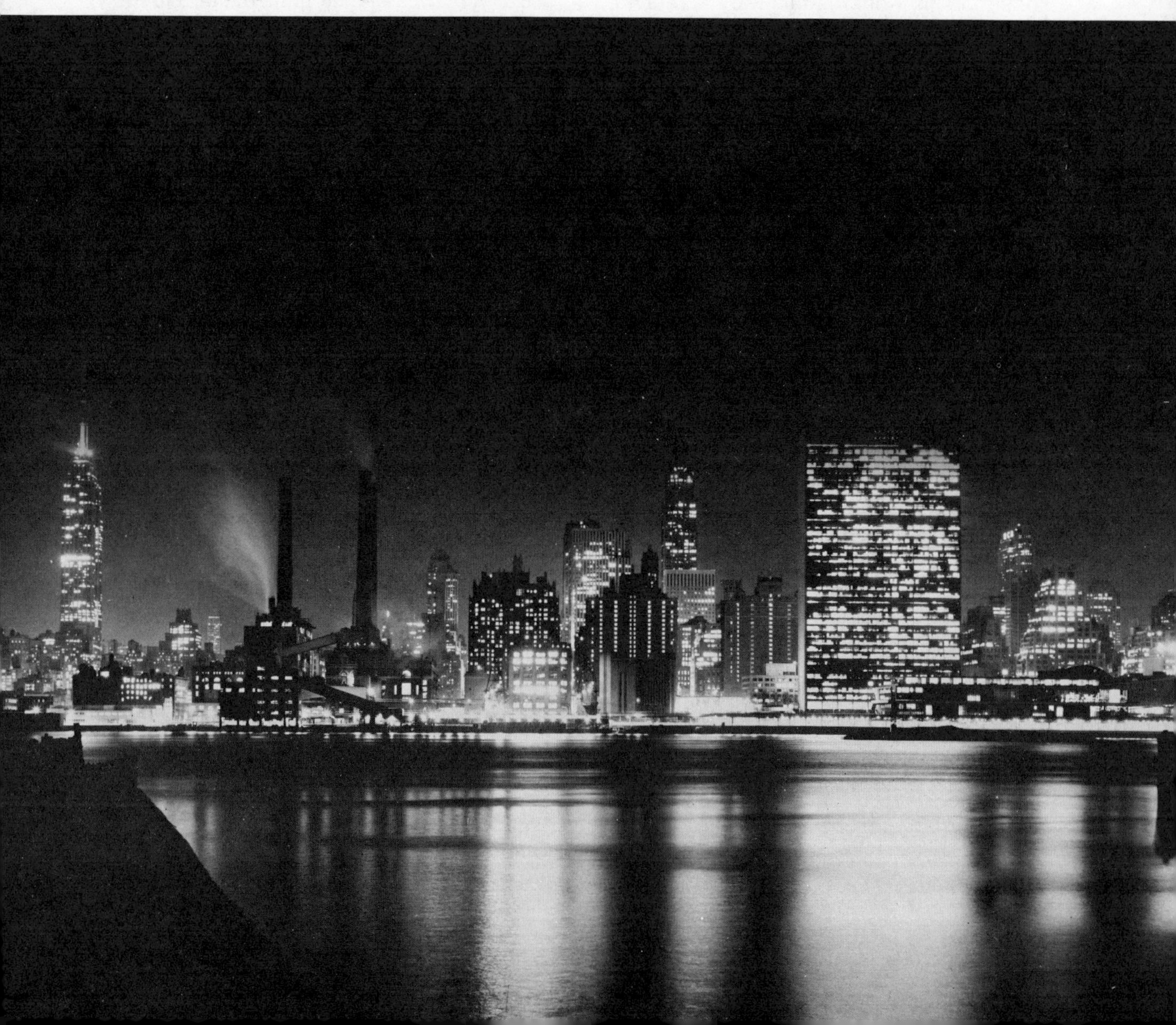

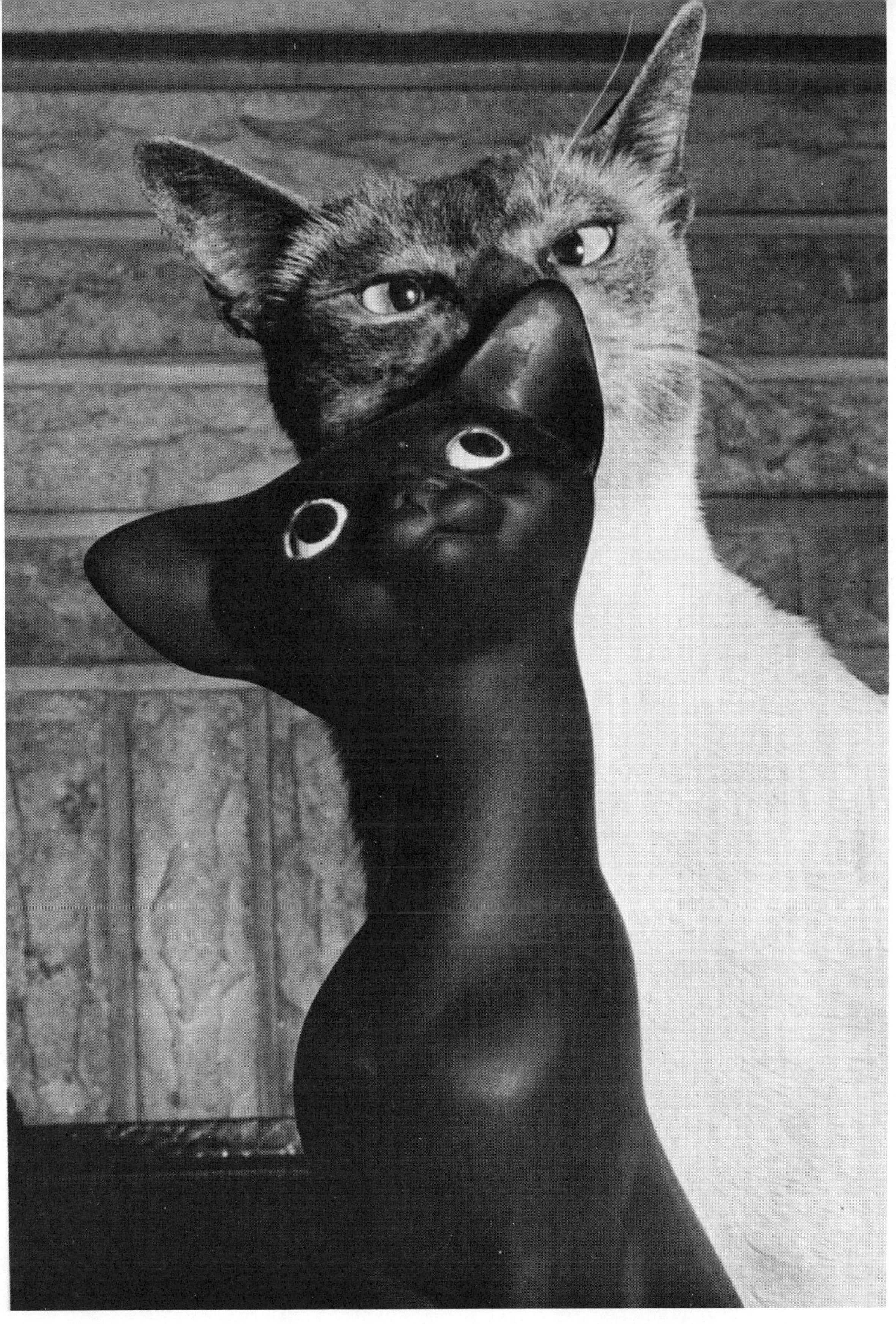

The Ayes Have It. Photo by Craig Cihlar.

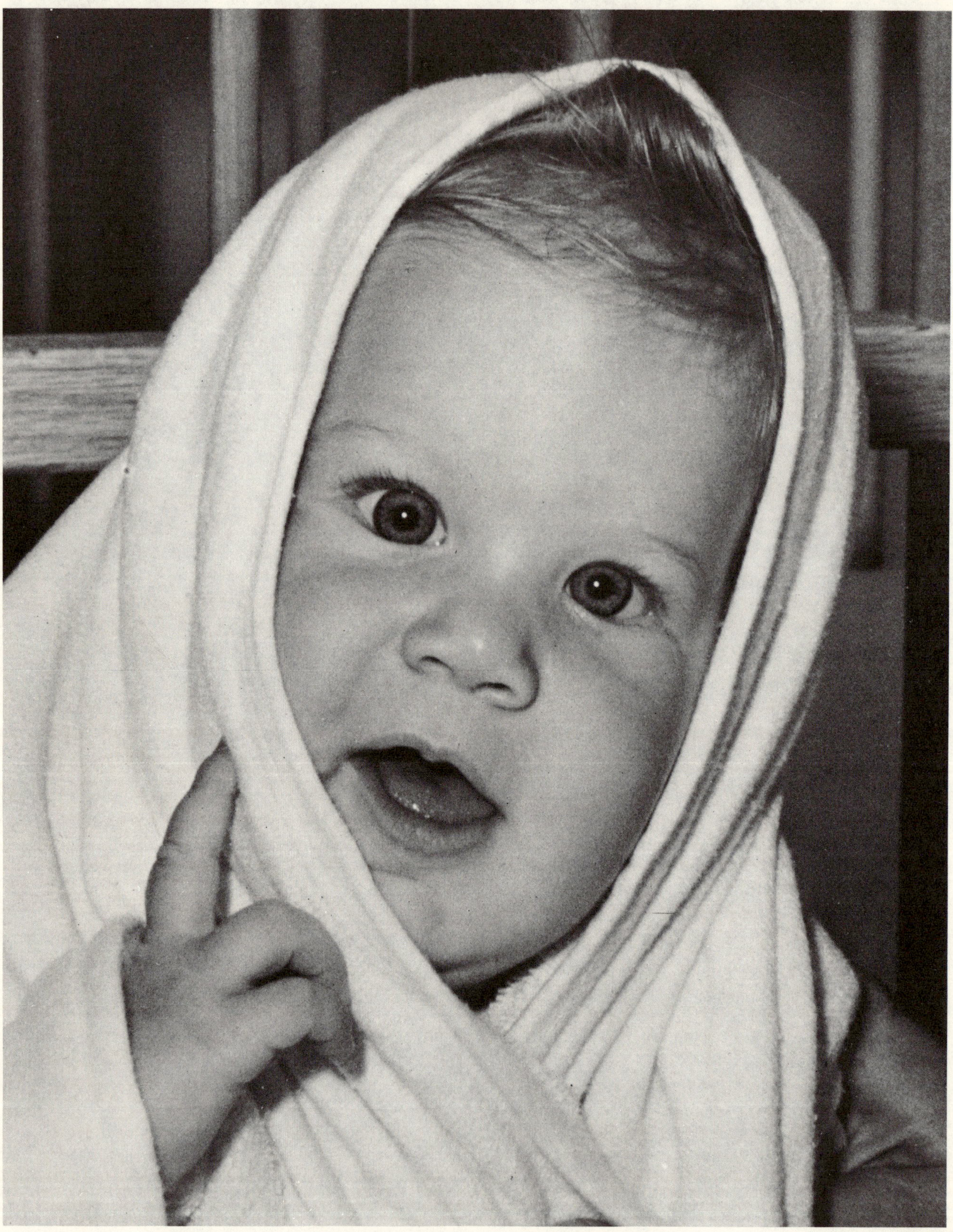

Donna. DXF.

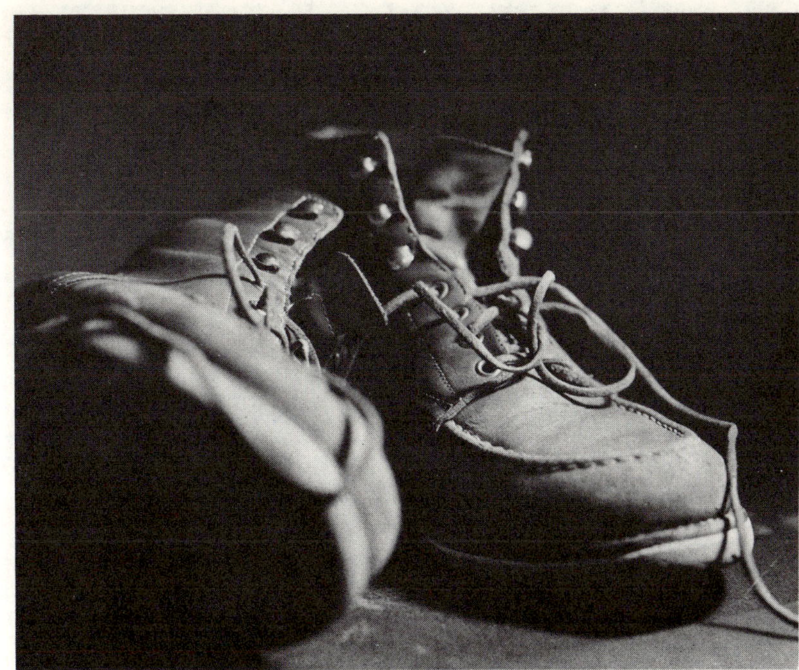

Old Shoes. Photo by Dave Greenwald.

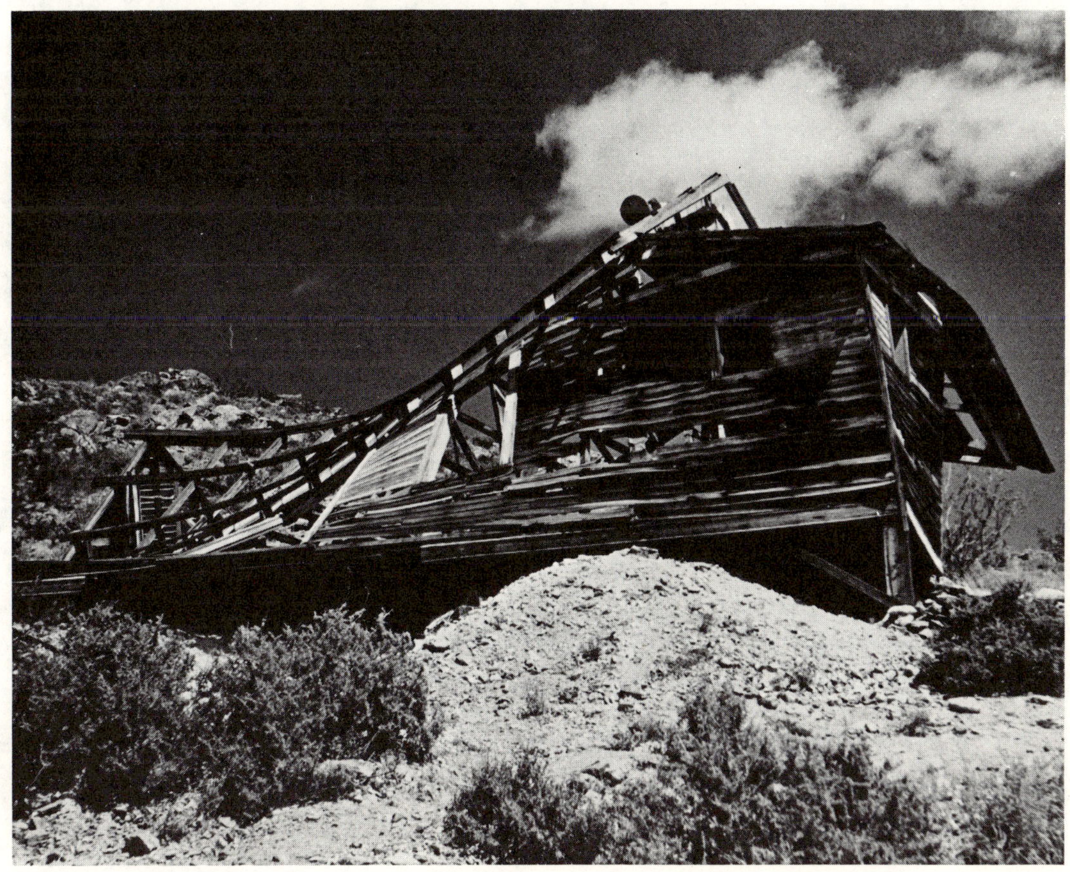

There Once Was a House. Photo by Linda Page.

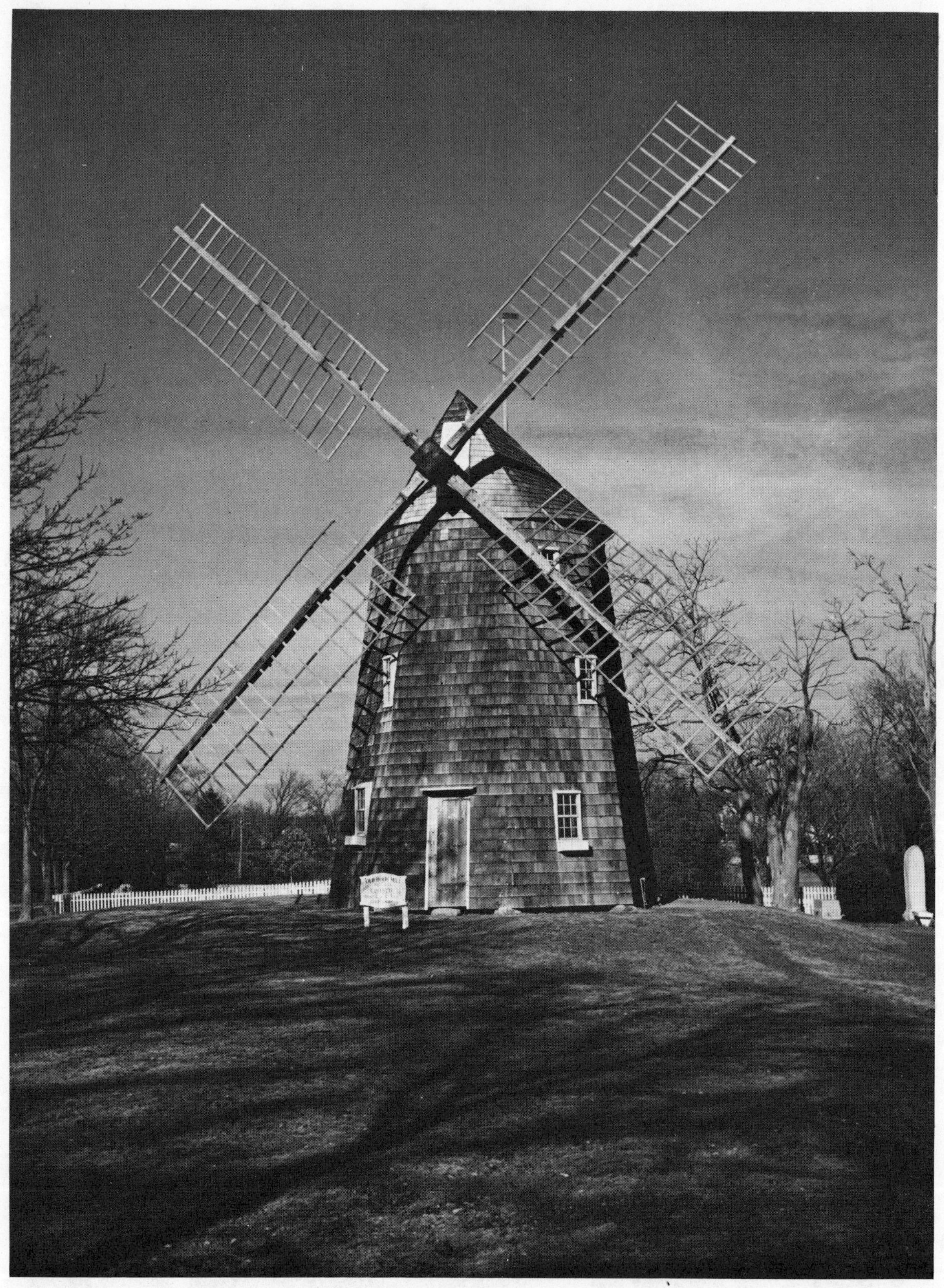

Old Mill. Photo by Laurence Van Wallendael.

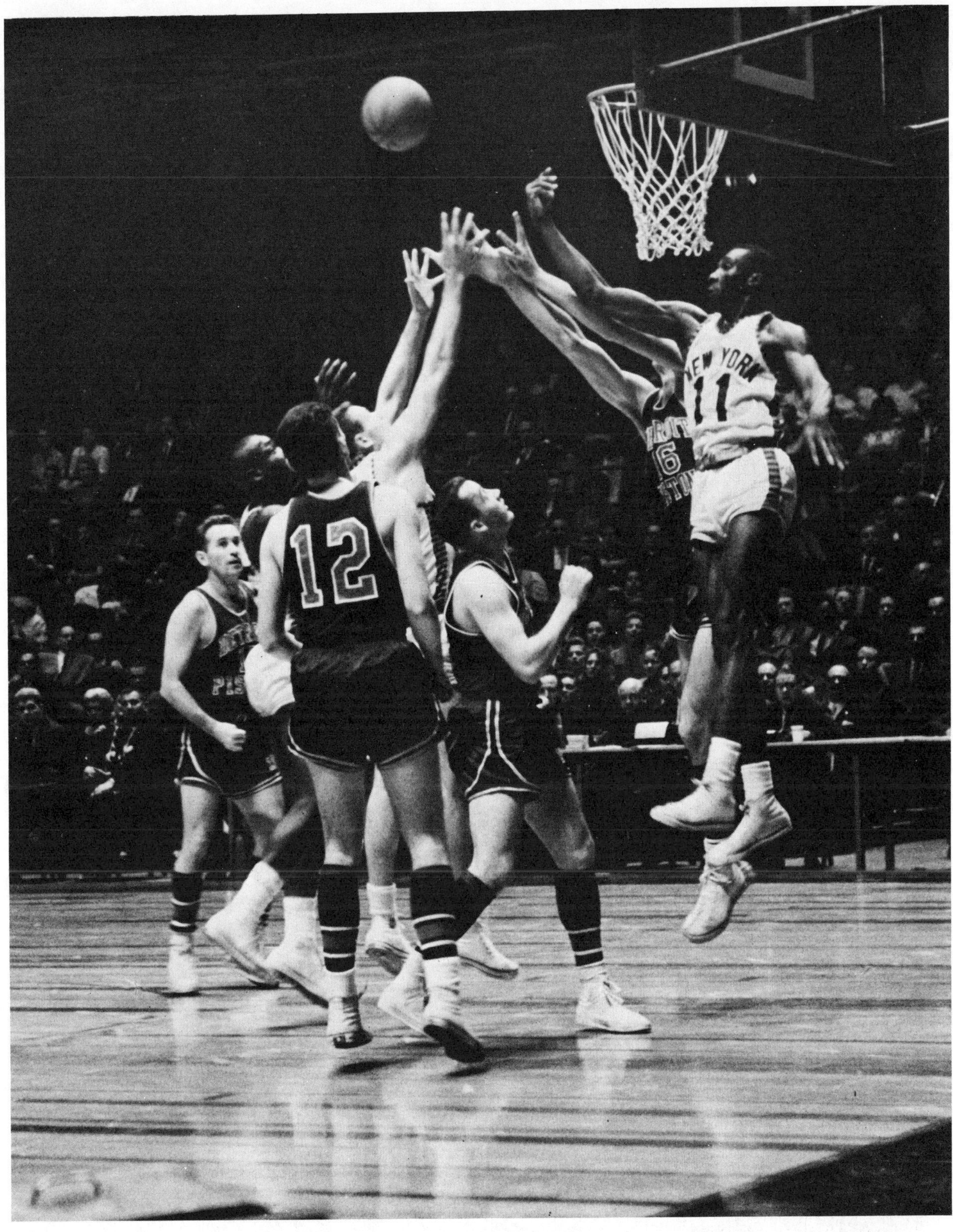

Reach! DXF.

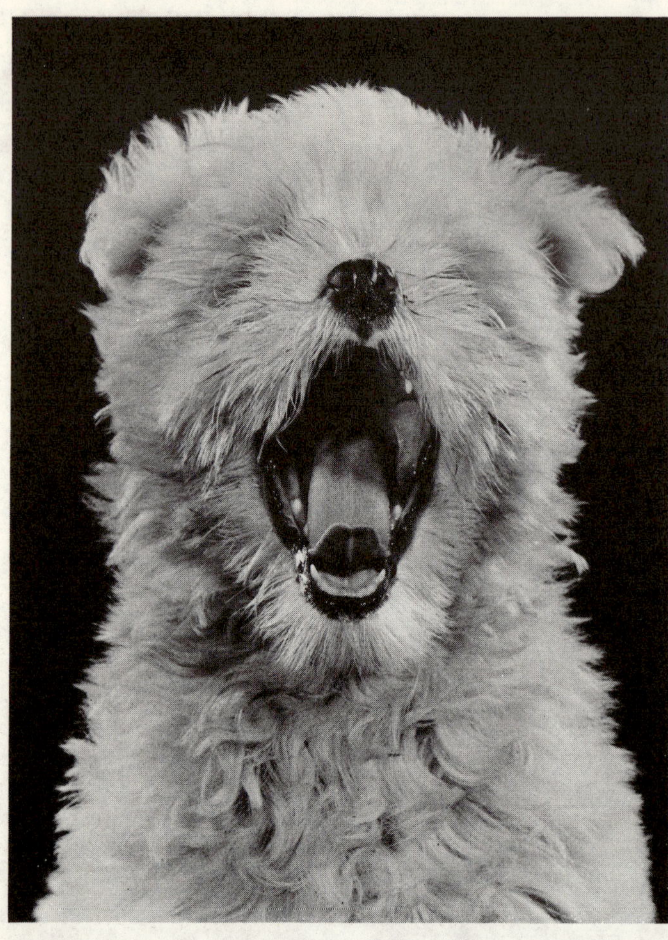

(Left) The Yawn. Photo by John Gajda. (Below) Hay Time. Photo by Virgil Coenen.

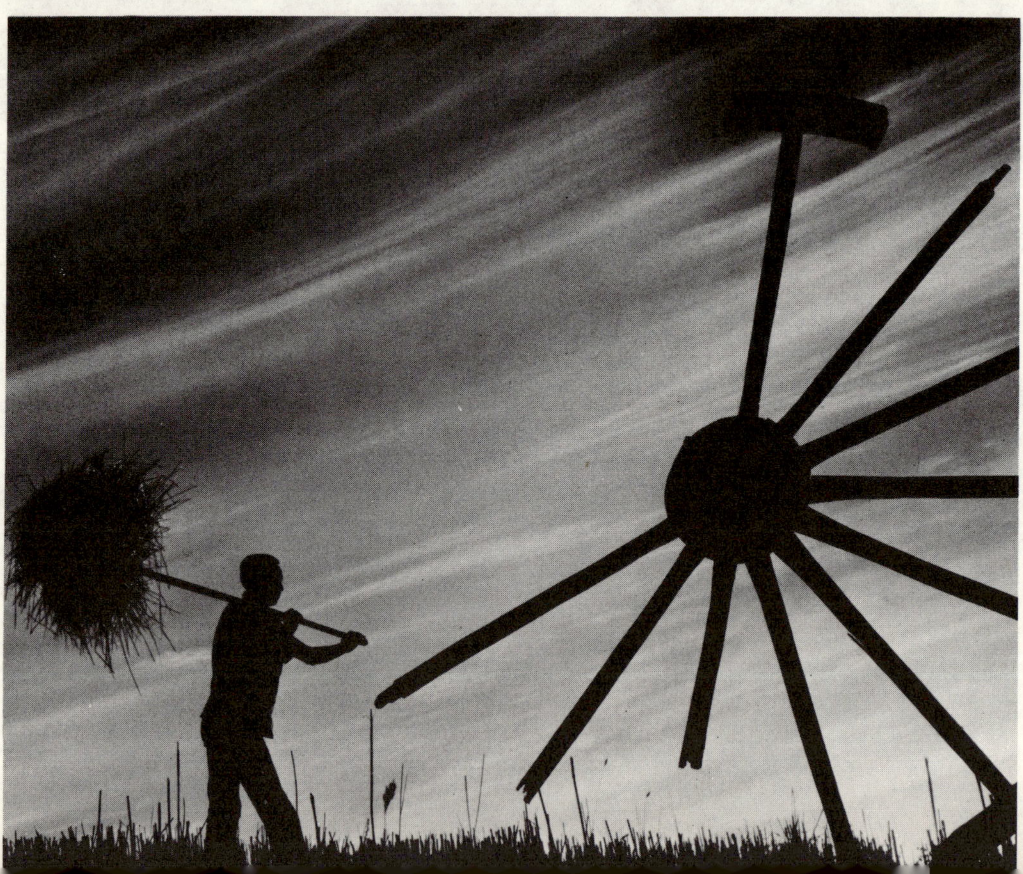

7

ACCESSORIES MAKE BETTER PHOTOS EASIER

Photography, it often seems, was invented for people who cannot resist the temptation apparently built into all gadgets. To aid and unburden these people, photographic equipment manufacturers have placed a wider variety of accessories and gadgets on the market than can be found in almost any other hobby. To make matters worse, just about every one of these accessories will help the photographer make better photos.

As in all things, a line must be drawn somewhere. On one side of this line are the items that are virtual necessities for better photographs, and on the other, the items it would be very nice to have after all the necessities are owned and you could afford to buy them "just for fun."

EXPOSURE METERS

High on the list of necessities, at least in my book, are exposure meters. Though it is true some professionals neither use them, nor indeed, seem to need them, this book is not designed for their use. For the most part, the amateur photographer lacks the experience and ability to "guesstimate" proper exposure correctly without the aid of an exposure meter.

Although most newer cameras have built-in exposure meters, even through-the-lens types, these are not infallible, especially under adverse lighting conditions. Many cameras, especially older ones, have no meter.

The two basic types of hand-held exposure meters, incident-light meters and reflected-light meters, have enough backers to make choosing between them difficult. The incident-light meters are held close to the subject and pointed at the camera to measure the intensity of total light falling on the subject. The reflected-light meters are pointed at the subject, to measure the amount of light reflected from the subject area. In use, the reflected-light method of exposure is considered more dependable for outdoor scenes, while the incident-light method is especially good for small objects out of doors, and for indoor pictures using artificial lights. Manufacturers give the photographer a choice, as a good many reflected-light meters have incident-light meter attachments as well.

No matter what type of meter you choose, it will be an invaluable aid in getting better photographs. To get the most from your meter, follow the instructions given in the manufacturer's instruction booklet. Use the meter for just about every exposure, indoors or out, and vary your position and holding angle to match the situation. In any event, be sure to check your meter readings with the results you get. If your readings tend to be too high or too low for a specific film, make the adjustment and remember this every time you use the film.

Exposure meters, when used correctly, will almost guarantee a perfectly exposed picture.

FLASH AND STROBE UNITS

While in the general field of light, its measurement and gauging for exposure, another photographic accessory must be considered. With the invention of the flashbulb, and its availability to photographers in the early 1930's, amateur photography took another giant step toward its current versatility.

As with almost everything else, time has

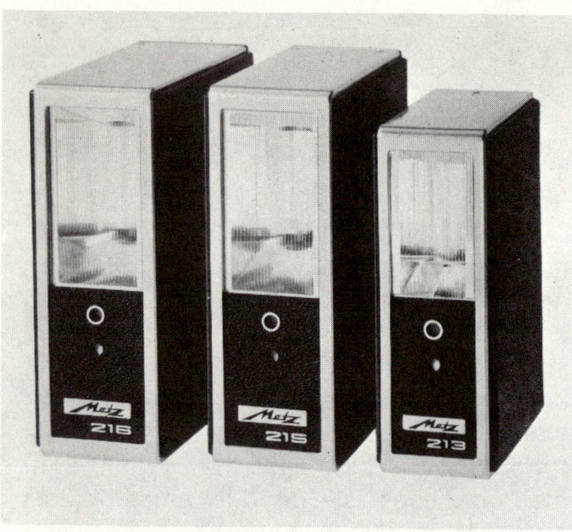

These small, powerful strobe units all have autoflash, which automatically gives you enough light for each situation.

brought its improvements—flash cubes have replaced bulbs on the simplest cameras, bulbs are now tiny, flashguns have become compact (and some fold), and electronic flash units (strobe lights) are now inexpensive enough for many amateurs.

To find the correct *f*/stop in flash photography, merely divide the guide number, found on the bulb container, by the distance between the flash and the subject. Using this result, find the closest corresponding *f*/stop on your camera. Shutter speed is determined by instructions on the bulb package or flash unit. This is the correct setting for the bulb and film combination. Here are a few things to keep in mind when using flash or strobe.

When buying flashbulbs, make sure you buy the type for which your camera is synchronized (or that your camera synchronization dial matches the bulb type). The wrong bulb or synchronization will result in improper meshing of bulb peak and open shutter, and your photo will be ruined.

56

Flash techniques are few and simple, all serving a specialized purpose. Those cameras which have the flash already attached allow an almost foolproof exposure technique. However, this very simplicity may provide a great disadvantage, giving the photo such even lighting that the tones are flat and uninteresting. Also, in this situation, if the subject is close to the background, a heavy black shadow will result. If you have a camera-flash combination of this type, remember to move your subject far enough away from the background so the entire area is in very dark shadow, instead of forming a distinct shadow pattern.

If your flash unit is detachable, try holding it high over your head and slightly to the side. This will give adequate light, while keeping some shadows on the side farthest from the flash, giving the natural illusion of roundness and depth.

For those cameras not synchronized for flash, use the open flash method. Set the camera on a steady support, preferably a tripod, with the shutter on time or bulb. Hold the flash unit in the desired position, open the camera shutter, fire the bulb, and quickly close the shutter. This must be done as quickly as possible to avoid getting a double image.

Flash stopped the action but made photo stark and unrealistic. Reflectors would have softened deep shadows. DXF.

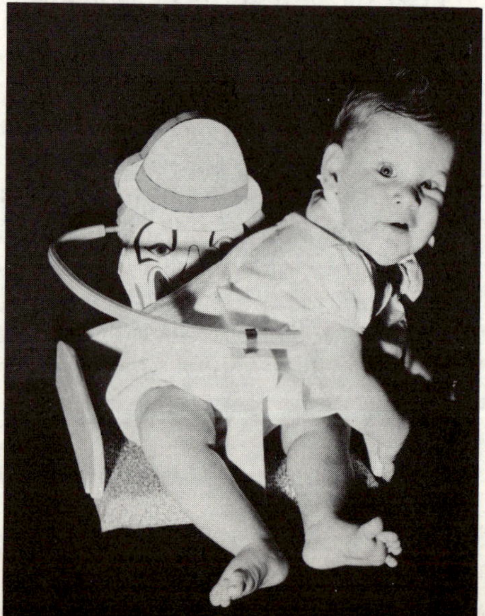

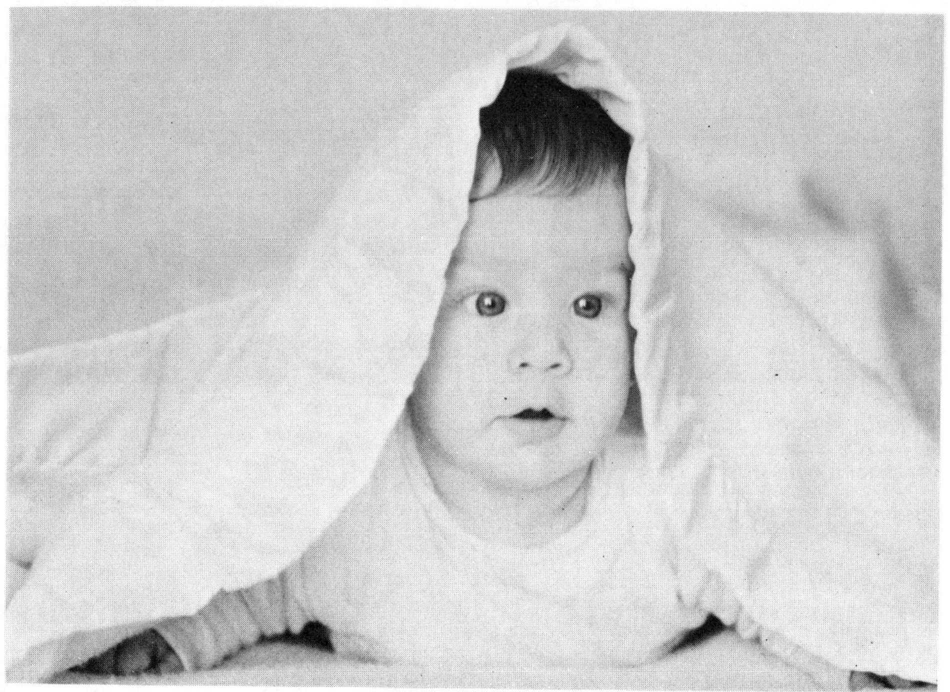

Strobe unit stopped expression cold, but because normal development time was used in producing negative, result was soft. DXF.

For a very soft, extremely pleasing flash photo, try the bounce flash technique. For this, the flashgun is aimed at the wall or ceiling to reflect or bounce light back onto the subject. To gauge exposure correctly, determine the distance from the unit to the ceiling to the subject, and divide by the guide number. This gives you the f/stop. Then, open up the lens 2½ stops to make up for the light lost bouncing around.

Another way to get soft results using a flashbulb is to remove the reflector from the flash unit and take the picture with the reflectorless flashgun. This is called the bare or reflectorless flash technique. With bare flash, open the lens an additional two stops or so, depending on the color of the room. Never use a bare flash on the camera—always away and off to one side.

If your camera has an "X" synchronization setting, you can use an electronic flash. These units, which are becoming less expensive and more in the range of the amateur, flash over and over again without the trouble and expense of replacing the bulb after every exposure. Usually utilizing AC house current and/or batteries, these units do not require any special filters for either color or black-and-white film. With their very short light duration, strobe units are excellent for stopping action. The rules for flashbulb use apply to strobe units, and the guide numbers for specified films can be found in the instruction booklets packed with the strobe units.

While flash and strobe units are described here mainly as important accessories for indoor photography, they may also be used for outdoor fill-flash. Used on the camera, the flash, combined with sunlight, will help in cases of extreme shadows caused by back- or sidelighting. Be careful not to use the full power of the bulb directly on the subject, for the flash will make it appear flat and shadowless. Instead, either move further away from the subject, or shield the flashgun by stretching a clean white handkerchief taut over the bulb.

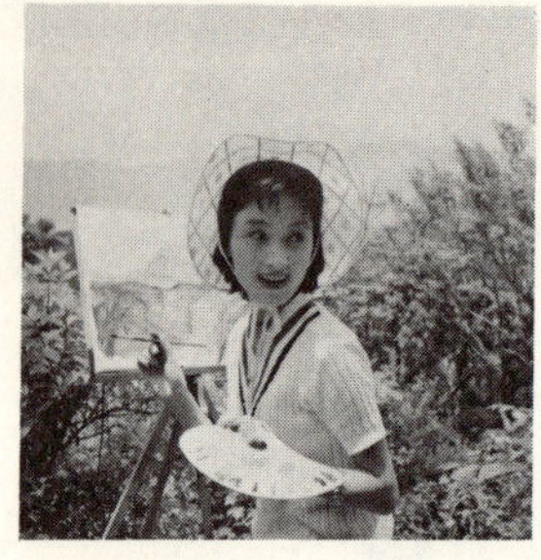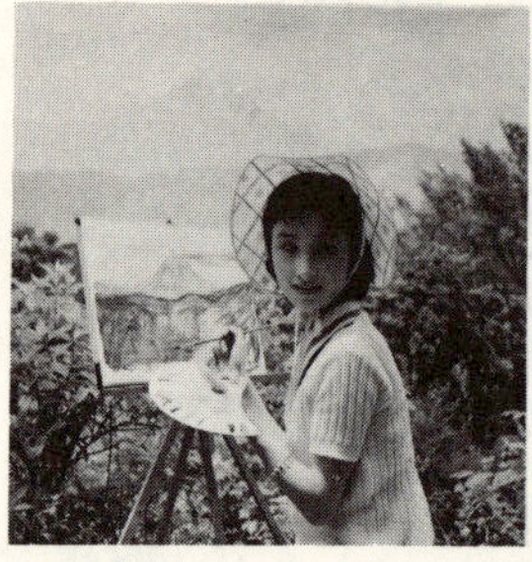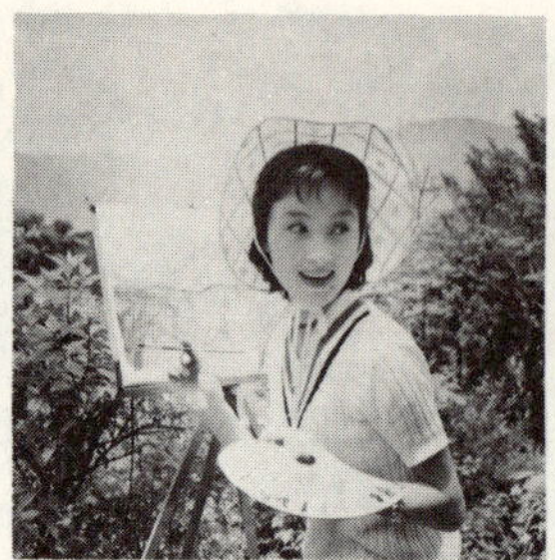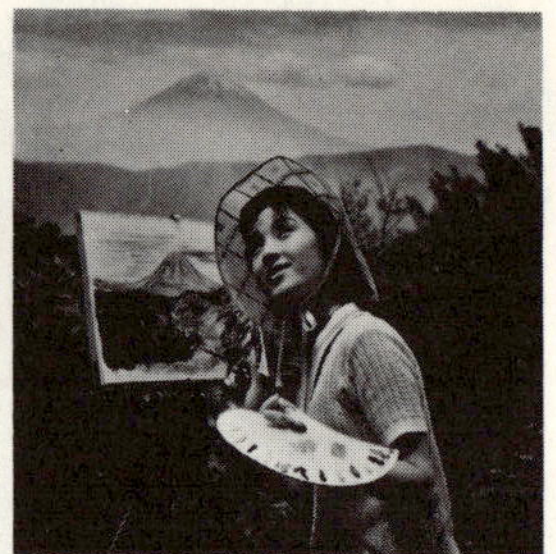

Photos taken under same conditions with (l to r) no filter, Walz medium yellow, light green, and red filters. Photo courtesy of Walz.

FILTERS

Filters are designed to keep out certain colors of light and admit others. Those available can help you get better pictures, and may actually make the difference between a very ordinary photo and a fine, dramatic shot.

For black-and-white photography, there are approximately 25 different kinds, colors, and intensities of filters available. Of these, three are really basic: yellow, green, and red. For the amateur, the most important filter is the yellow, preferably a medium yellow. The yellow filter makes sky blue darker, while accentuating the whiteness of the clouds.

The light green filter keeps sky colors normal while brightening greens, which tend to reproduce darker on film. This filter should also be used for outdoor portraits, for it will give a more normal skin tone than the medium yellow. The red filter is used for very dramatic shots only, and should be used sparingly. This filter could be used, for example, when photographing buildings or objects against the sky. A red filter turns sky blue to black, making the clouds leap forward in bold relief. It also makes green considerably darker, adding to the dramatic impact of the picture. The red filter should not be used for portraits, as it will distort skin tones badly, making them ghostly.

Since the very purpose of a filter is to hold back specific colors or intensities of light, a certain amount of exposure compensation must be added. For example, when using a medium yellow filter with black-and-white film, increase exposure one stop, with a light green filter increase two stops, and with a red filter increase three stops. The specific increases (''filter factors'') may be found in film and filter instruction sheets.

Remember to check your camera instruction booklet for the lens size or series number before buying filters. While some lenses will accept screw-in filters, others require an adapter ring. The adapter ring screws or attaches to the lens, holding the filter in place in front of the lens with a retaining ring.

Filters for color film are also available, but these are for more subtle tinting corrections. The most widely used filters in color work are the skylight or haze filters. These are used to eliminate some of the atmospheric haze which, although usually invisible to the eye, is easily recorded by the camera lens. Polarizing filters are also available for color films, but the photographer should be thoroughly familiar with their properties before buying or using them.

LENS SHADE

Your lens shade should be purchased at the same time as your camera. These relatively inexpensive hoods can and do save more pictures from being ruined than their low price would indicate. Since the lens shade protects the lens from any direct light rays, especially when dealing with side- or backlighted shots, it should be left on the camera, and used for both indoor and outdoor photography.

TRIPOD

For several photographic situations, a tripod becomes a must. If you cannot hold your camera absolutely steady for a sharp, clear picture with a shutter speed of 1/50 sec., a tripod would prove invaluable. For longer exposures, or for any exposure with a telephoto or heavy zoom lens, a tripod is necessary to prevent camera movement after releasing the shutter.

No matter what the occasion, it is almost universal that pictures include everybody but the photographer. The tripod can help remedy this situation. By prefocusing the camera, set solidly on the tripod, the photographer can set the self-timer and move toward the group. He has plenty of time to walk into the setting and be part of the picture. While not an absolute necessity, a tripod is a very useful and important accessory.

LENSES

Heading the list of accessories it would be very nice to have should be extra lenses. These lenses—close-up, auxiliary, and interchangeable lenses—add greatly to the versatility of any camera, simple or complex. With these lenses, the photographer can get close-ups where they might otherwise be impossible, often without sacrificing the anonymity of candid camera work.

Close-up lenses are available for almost any camera, permitting extreme close-ups when used in conjunction with the normal camera lens. When using close-up lenses, which resemble clear filters, as well as other additional lenses, you must focus very accurately, and allow for parallax correction with non-reflex cameras, since the depth of field becomes very shallow. Even the slightest error in focusing can result in a fuzzy picture. With some of the larger telephoto lenses, for example, the depth of field extends only the distance between nose tip and ear, on a portrait. You can see why very sharp focusing becomes essential.

Auxiliary lenses are available for certain cameras for both telephoto and wide-angle work, and are considerably less expensive than the large interchangeable type. On those cameras which do not have the capability of lens interchangeability, these lenses, used in conjunction with the camera's normal lens, offer a measure of versatility for a very small price. Again, as with the close-up lenses, these auxiliary units de-

Interchangeable Nikkor lenses, including wide-angle, super-speed, and telephoto.

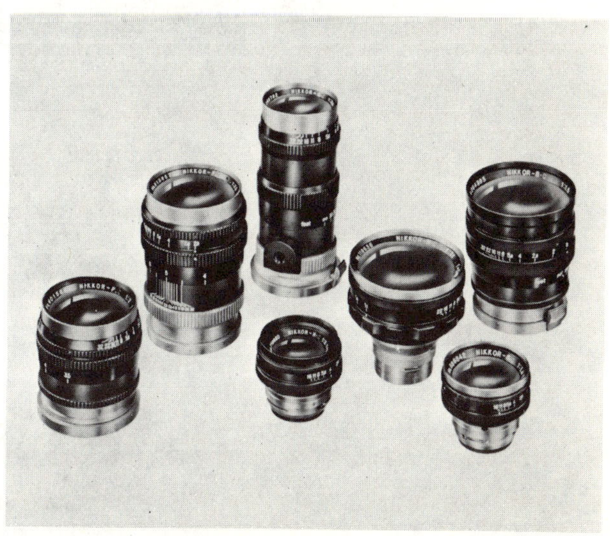

mand care in parallax correction and focusing, for best results.

Telephoto and wide-angle lenses for the interchangeable-lens camera are the last word in versatility. For 35mm cameras, they can be as long as 2000mm telephotos or as short as 8 or 10mm "fisheye" wide-angles (normal is about 50mm). These lenses allow the photographer to pick out a single face in a crowd, bring far-off objects closer, or capture the total environment of a scene. Despite their cost, and the precision required in adjusting focus, they more than pay for themselves in increased versatility and picture-taking latitude, as well as in plain fun.

Photos taken with 25mm wide-angle, 50mm normal, 135mm telephoto, and 500mm telephoto Nikkor lenses.

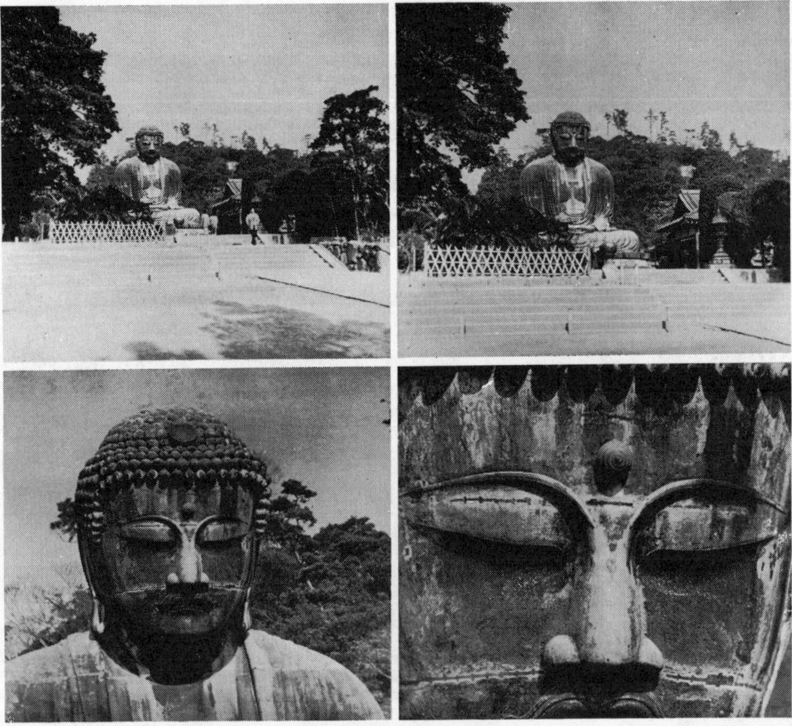

CAMERA COMPANION

For pocket use fold on lines 7 and 24

TYPE OF FILM.. ASA #................ B & W ☐ COLOR ☐

Date Purchased................ Date Processed....................by................

EXP	SUBJECT	DATE	f STOP	SPEED	TYPE OF LIGHT	FLASH TYPE	FILTER	REMARKS
1								
2								
3								
4								
5								
6								
7								
8								
9								
10								
11								
12								
13								
14								
15								
16								
17								
18								
19								

*Record sheets, if kept accurately, will help
amateurs avoid the same mistake twice.*

MISCELLANEOUS

A description of all the available accessories, and how they can help you take better photos, could easily fill not only the remainder of this book, but a second volume as well. So the author will take the liberty of selecting the few he would choose and telling why.

1. Gadget bag—should be of good size and sturdy construction. This bag will then hold all the gadgets and accessories we have convinced ourselves we *really* need.

2. Self-timer—allows the photographer the luxury of appearing on the other side of the camera. The timers give the photographer up to 30 seconds to get from behind the camera into posing position, before setting off the shutter. Many cameras, even inexpensive ones, have this feature built in.

3. Cable release—helps eliminate camera movement when you snap the shutter and is ideal for exposures made with the camera set on a tripod.

4. Blower brush—when used frequently and properly, this will keep dust and lint off the lens and camera. It combines a fine sable brush with a blower bulb to do a complete cleaning job.

5. Record sheets—designed to help you check exposure, film, and speed against photo results. Their purpose is to make sure you do not make the same mistake twice.

These are but a few of the gadgets available Besides all these used for cameras, there are many for developing, printing, and enlarging.

Again, before buying any of these accessories, be sure to check your camera manual for correct size, type, and any other pertinent information. Decide whether you really need this gadget, or whether its cost outweighs its usefulness. Buy only the accessories you are sure you will use often. Professionals only buy what they know they can and will use to improve their pictures. Emulation will improve your pictures and save you money.

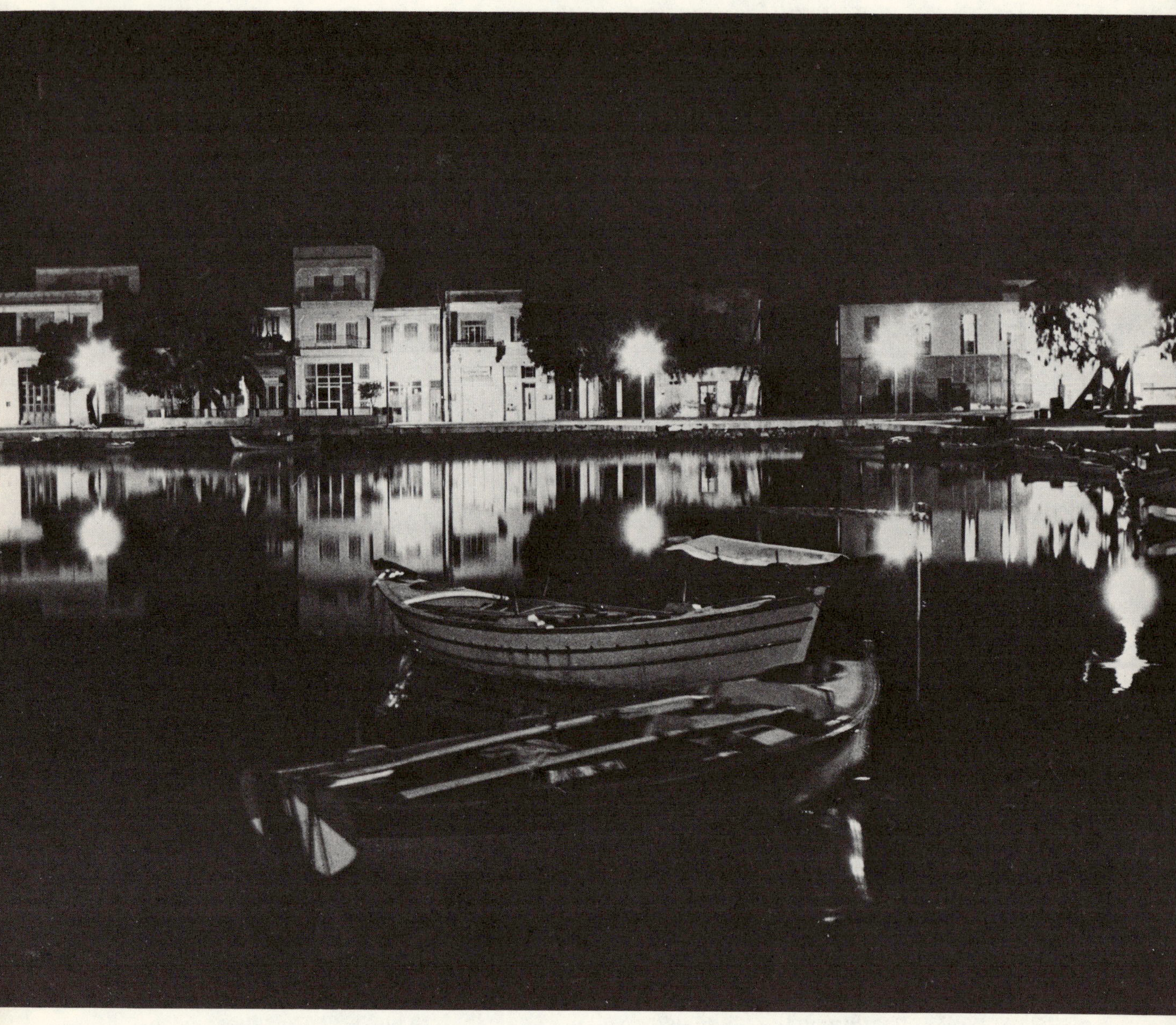

A long exposure was required to make this shot of the fishing harbor at Ayios Nikolaos, Crete. As a result, the boat in the foreground is slightly blurred. Photo by Herb Taylor.

SPECIAL TECHNIQUES FOR SPECIAL SHOTS

Many of us labor under the misconception that there are certain conditions under which good photography is extremely difficult. This may have been true 75, 50, 25, or even 10 years ago. However, it is not true today. The combination of fine, fast lenses and super-speed films presently available make good photography relatively simple under even the most exacting conditions. In fact, it can safely be said, a photographer can take fine pictures under some of the most adverse lighting conditions. Of course, special techniques are required for these situations, but "special" does not necessarily mean difficult. Rather, these techniques merely require more practice.

PHOTOGRAPHY AT NIGHT

One of these "specials" is the idea, long held by amateurs, that outdoor night photography is for professionals only. A few simple steps, coupled with several hints and suggestions, and you can not only take pictures at night, but you can take very good ones.

For a fighting chance at a decent picture taken outdoors at night, select a fast film, Ilford HP4, Tri-X, or one even faster in black-and-white, and for color, at least GAF 200 and 500 Color Slide films or Kodak High Speed Ektachrome (ASA 160). If at all possible, just as at other times, take a meter reading. Sensitive meters, or meters made more sensitive through the use of booster cells, will record in places where a reasonable amount of light is present. This includes a floodlit area, theater marquee, or storefront. If the needle won't budge, even with the booster, there is little left to do but experiment. This is where practice comes in.

Try this as a starting point. With the camera mounted securely on a tripod, and with a cable release to eliminate vibrations, expose Tri-X film for one second at $f/2.8$, for a night scene with reasonably good light. Expose for 10 seconds for poorly lit scenes and at least one minute for very badly lit scenes. Correspondingly longer exposures should be made when using slower film. While it is true these suggestions should only get you a photograph, it is primarily your own experience gained from experimenting and bracketing shots that will get you really good exposures. Once you have determined the correct exposure for certain conditions, jot it down so it will be available next time you need it, and can be used for comparison with the resultant photos.

When you have perfected this technique, learn ways to get better photographs. Use a lens shade to keep out stray light. Also, do not try to hand-hold the camera for long exposures. A sturdy tripod and cable release should be used to eliminate camera movement. Should car headlights come toward the camera during the exposure, cover the lens with your hat or coat, taking care not to touch the camera, and then, as soon as they pass, resume the exposure. Do not worry if a person should walk quickly in front of the camera. The image probably will not show on the developed film.

AVAILABLE LIGHT

We could call this branch of photography "making the most (and a little bit more) out of what you have." As mentioned previously, fast lenses, some as fast as $f/1.1$, combined with ultra-high-speed films, allow the photographer to get good results even un-

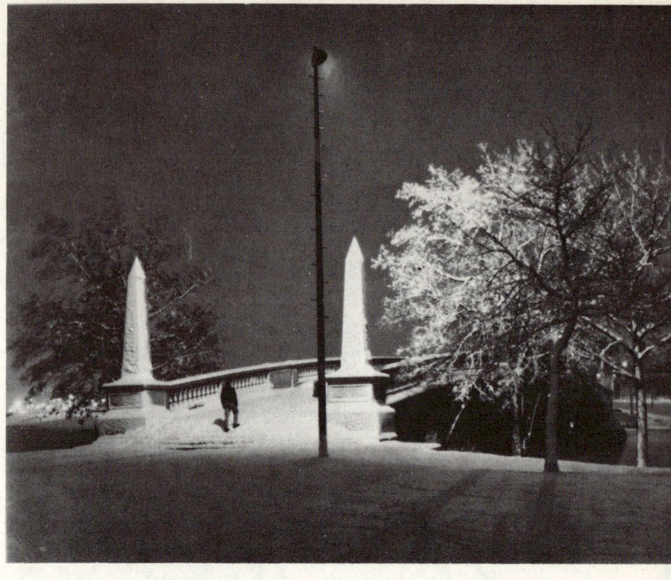

Night shot taken with Polaroid Land camera at EV 17 and exposed for two seconds. Photo by Nick Dean.

der the most adverse, dark, lighting conditions, without the aid of flash or strobe. In this area, candid photography really has come of age, since it requires no intrusion upon the privacy of the subject. The light on the scene, or available, is all that is used. There are no blinding flashbulbs or floodlights, and often you can relax, taking as many candid shots as you choose, without the subject being aware he is being photographed. This is especially useful when photographing a child.

For the best available light photography, make several decisions before you buy film and take pictures. First, what are you going to do with the negatives? Will your prints be small or relatively large? Will you sacrifice depth of field for additional lens aperture? Can you tolerate excessive grain? Your answers to these questions determine the speed of the film to use, and then the lens opening.

Most available lighting conditions are duck soup for a film like Kodak's Plus-X. Enlargements up to at least 11″ x 14″ do not show objectionable graininess, even when made from 35mm negatives. Faster black-and-white films and fast color films are excellent for available light photography, but do not use any faster film than is necessary. As noted before, the slower the film that can do the job, the better the results. The ultra-high-speed films tend toward graininess, causing you to lose some of the natural appearance of available light photography.

A great danger in available light photography is reluctance to trust the exposure meter, and the inability to resist the temptation to open it up "just a little bit" because, to us, the room seems so dark. We buy these meters and guides as aids, so we should trust them. Ignoring them leads to over- or underexposure.

Another very important contributor to the success or failure of available light pictures is the developing. Camera, film, and developing are each important as single parts, but they are also interdependent. Slow film plus slow lens plus "beefed-up" developer, can be as bad as fast film, fast lens, and wrong developer. If you do your own developing and printing, investigate the film-developer combinations, experiment, and then choose one. Vary it to fit different situations. When sending film to be processed, be sure to note the ASA rating at which you exposed it if it was not the "normal" one, so the processing organization knows the necessary developer and timing. It is not the best idea to send films which require special processing to the corner drugstore for gang processing. Many professional processing organizations are available near your home. Let them develop your film by inspection, rather than as one of a bunch. It may cost a bit more, but in the long run, if it saves a potentially good roll of film from being spoiled, it is well worth it.

A subject as broad, interesting, and important as this, requires a complete book for adequate coverage and discussion. *Night Photography Simplified*, by the Amphoto Editorial Board, is highly recommended.

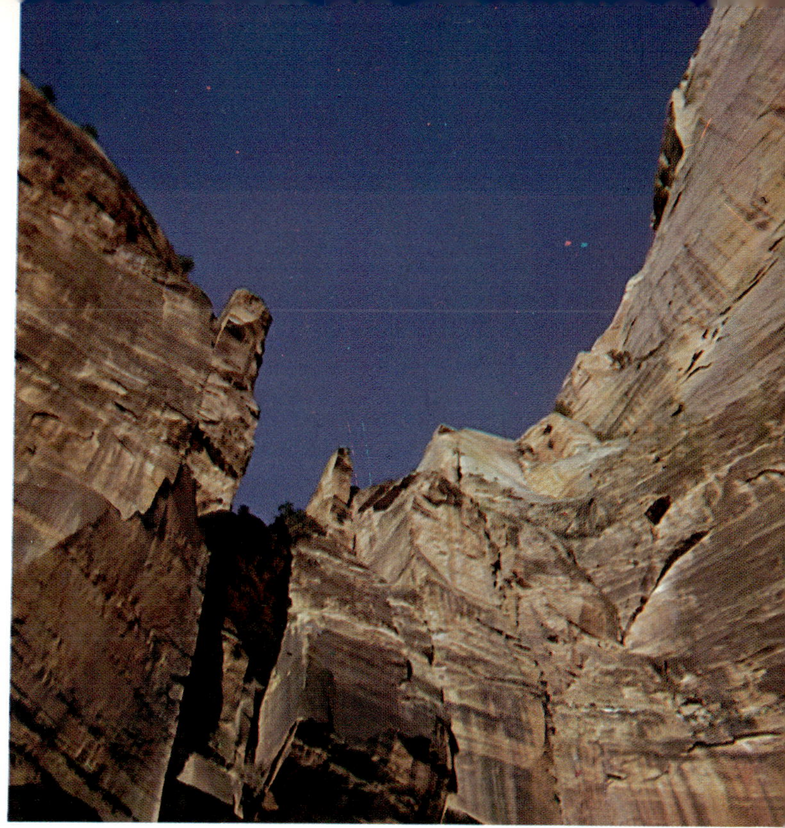

(Right) The bulk of rock against the sky emphasizes the dramatic impact of a low camera angle. Look around—the best pictures are often those improved by a different camera position. (Below) Placing the horizon line near the middle of the picture increases the peaceful atmosphere of this vivid sunset.

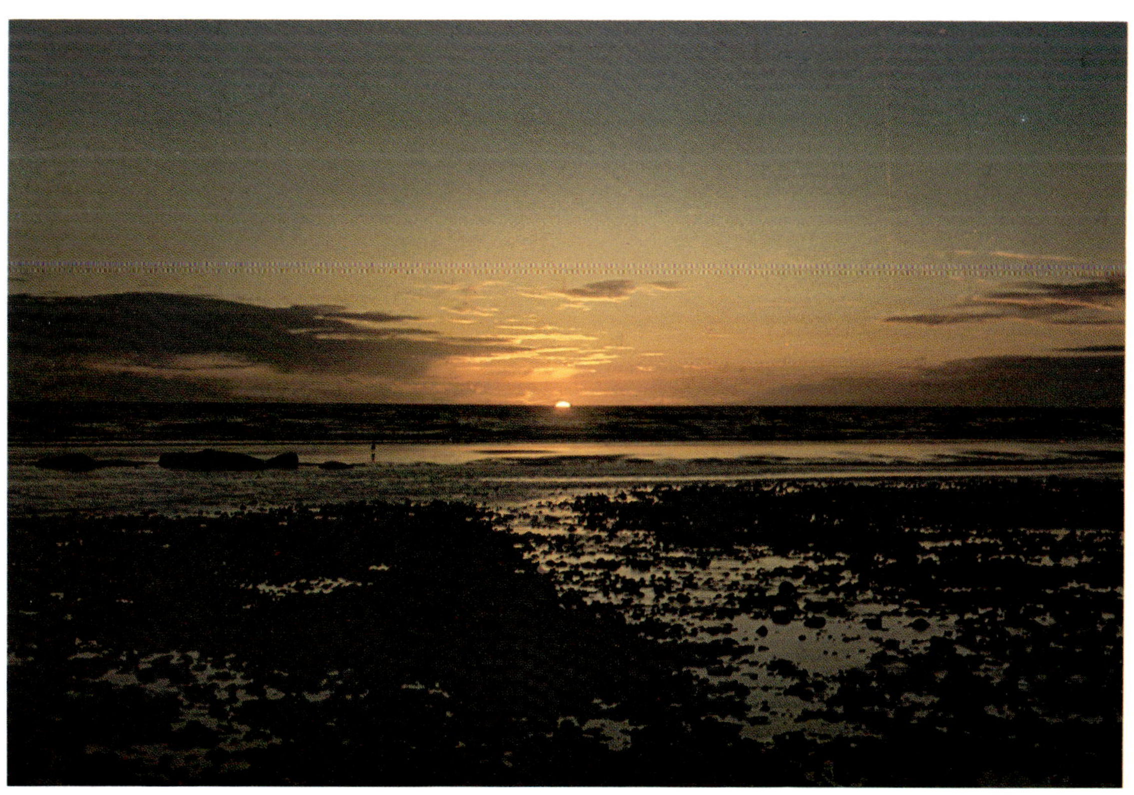

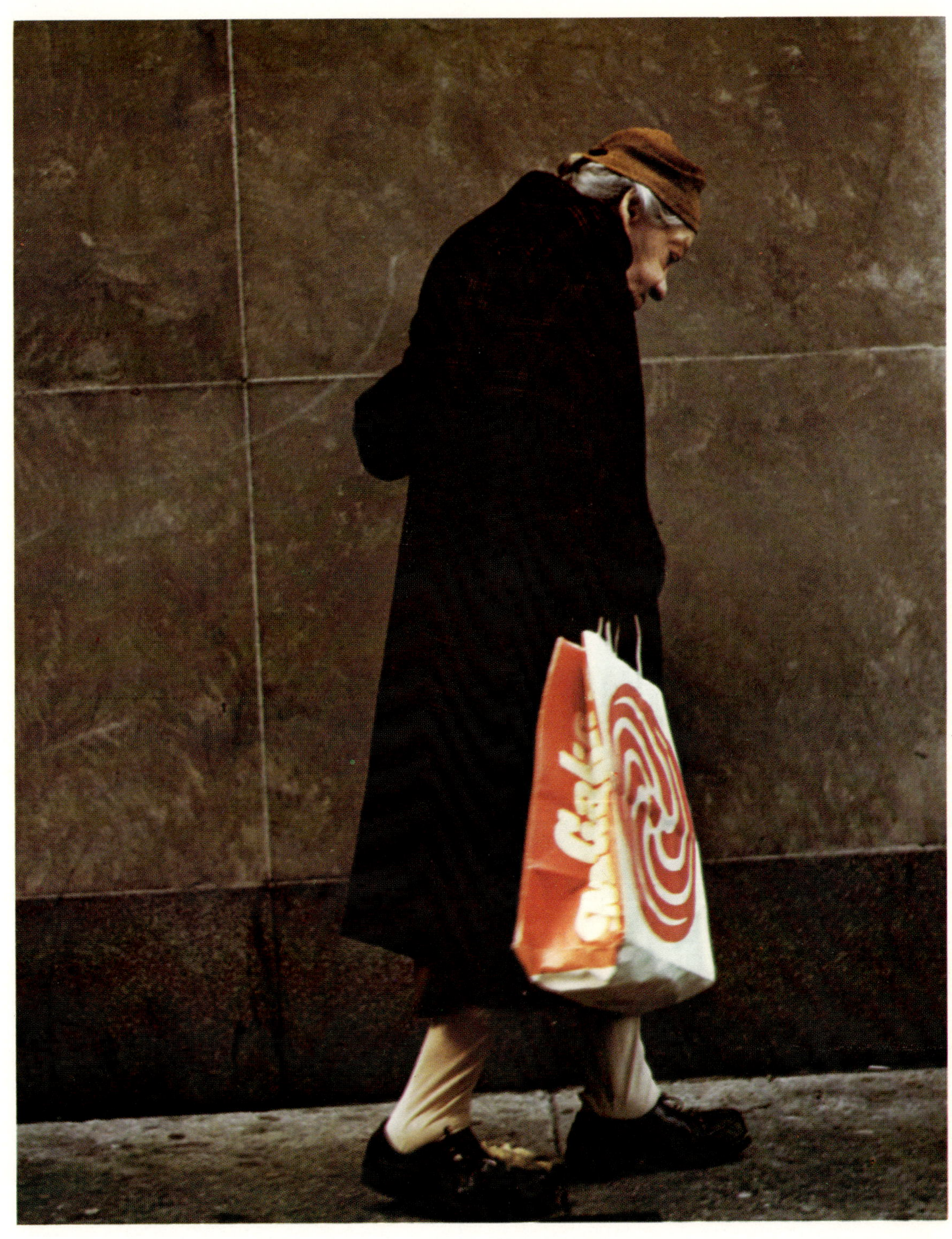

Old Age. The one touch of color points up the depressing aura of drabness in this street scene.

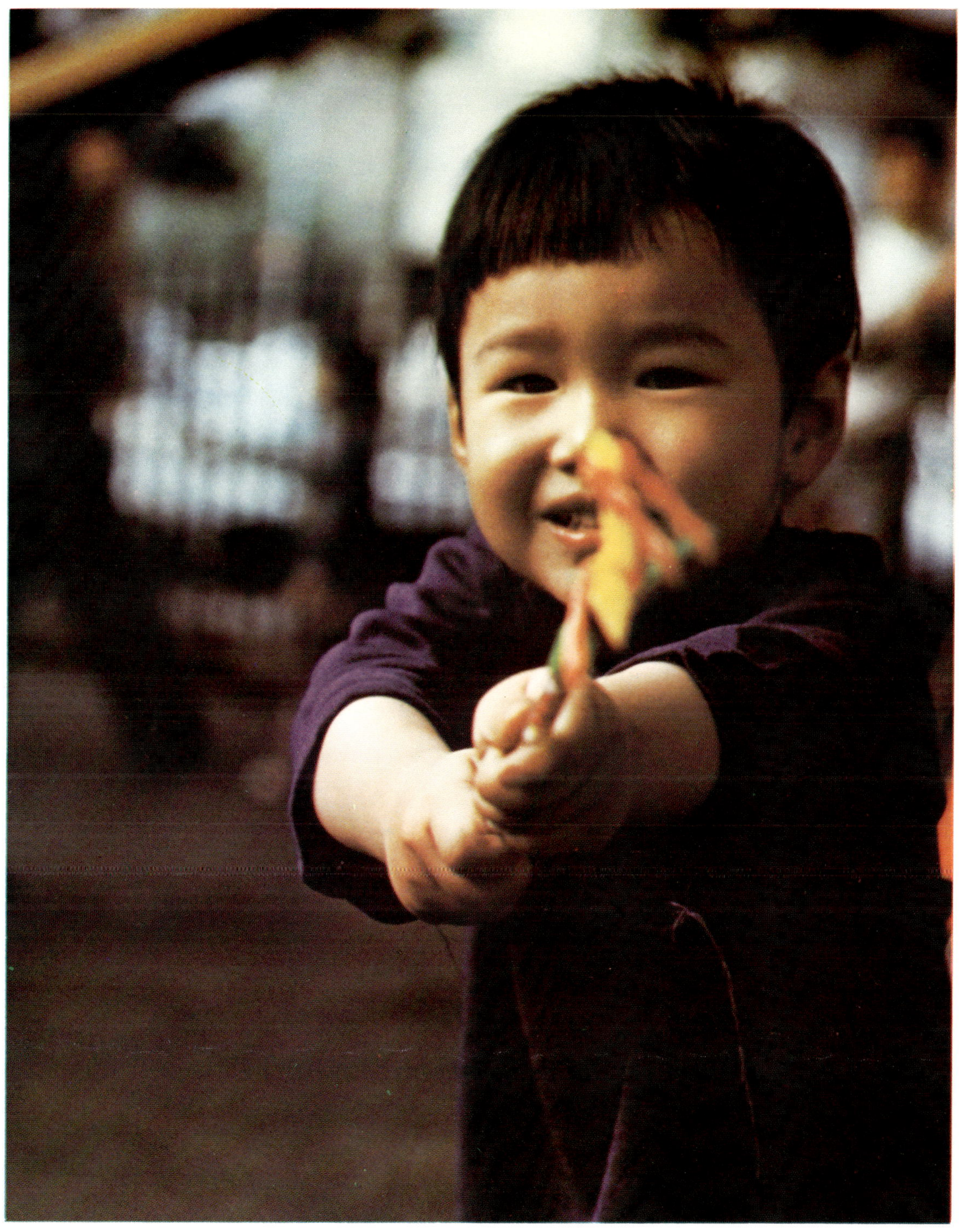

Youth. The best way to photograph children is to get low, down on their height level.

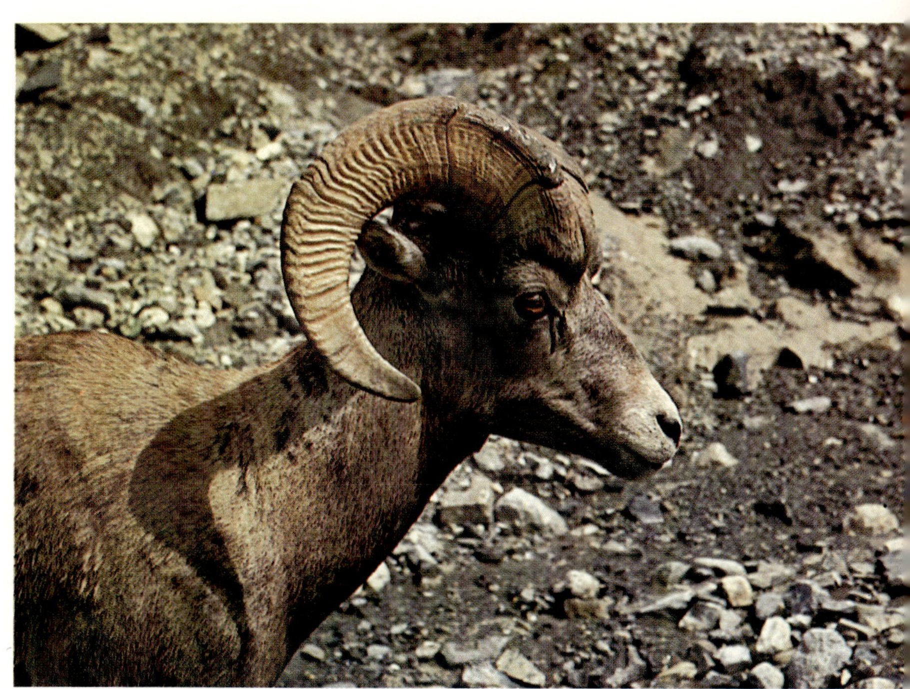

The great outdoors. (Right) The advantage of a telephoto lens is plain in this shot, as is its characteristic compression of backgrounds. (Below) A polarizing filter with color film darkens and intensifies the blue of the sky. To set it off, waiting for the ''right'' clouds to appear will improve the scene.

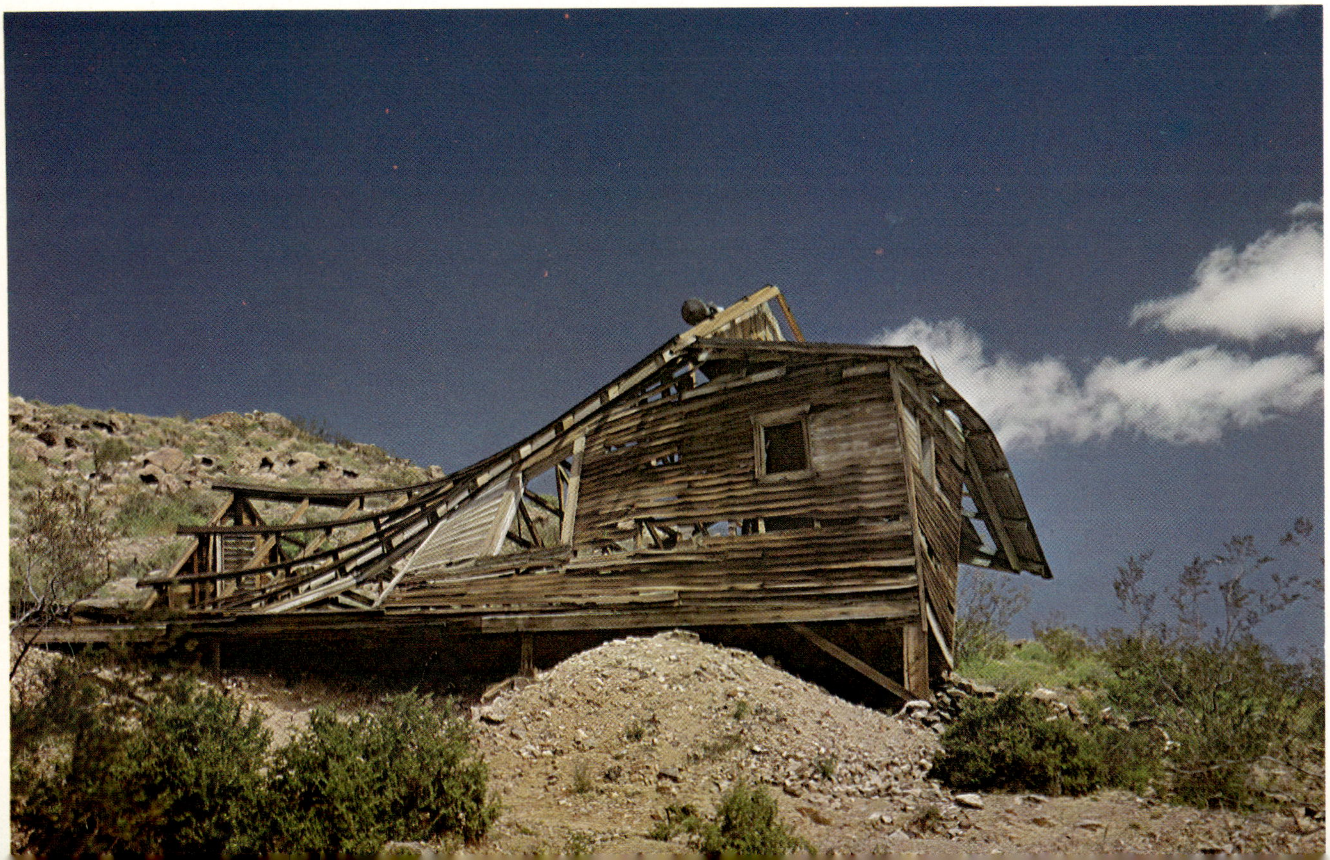

SPORTS AND ACTION PHOTOGRAPHY

When you record action, do you want to freeze it entirely, or do you prefer a slight blur to show the speed of the movement? Your own adaptation of the following hints will provide you with your preference.

It would be foolish to say any camera can take fine action shots. Instead, let us realize that the faster the shutter speed of the camera, the better is the chance of stopping the action clearly and sharply. Any camera with a top shutter speed of at least 1/100 sec. can be used for action photographs. However, you cannot depend entirely upon the camera to do the job. The relative speed of the object must also be considered. It should be noted that action can be stopped sharply by using flashbulbs, or even better, a strobe unit. However, since most of us rarely get within the 30-foot radius, necessary for flash and strobe, at sporting events and the like, this discussion is based on using no flash or strobe to stop reasonably fast action.

As far as the camera is concerned, moving objects at some distance from the camera do not move as quickly as similar objects near to the camera. Therefore, a slower shutter speed may be used for distant shots. Objects moving across the lens require considerably faster shutter speeds than those moving directly toward or away from the lens.

To further help your camera freeze action and get better sports and action photographs, a few additional hints are offered. Learn about the action you wish to photograph and anticipate the full action. Most actions reach a peak point, which is the perfect time to snap the photo. Picture a jumper in the air—the peak moment is achieved when he reaches his highest point and hesitates there for a split second before coming down. You must anticipate the peak and shoot just before it, so the small portion of a second required to activate the camera will coincide with the split-second pause at the peak of action.

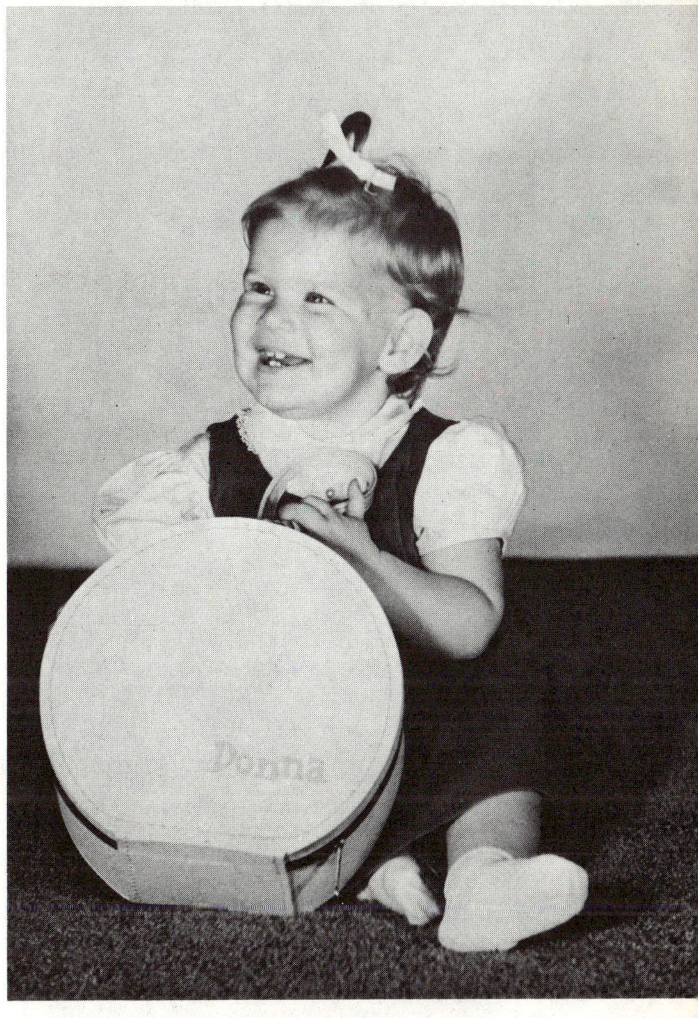

Available light and patience help capture a happy subject. DXF.

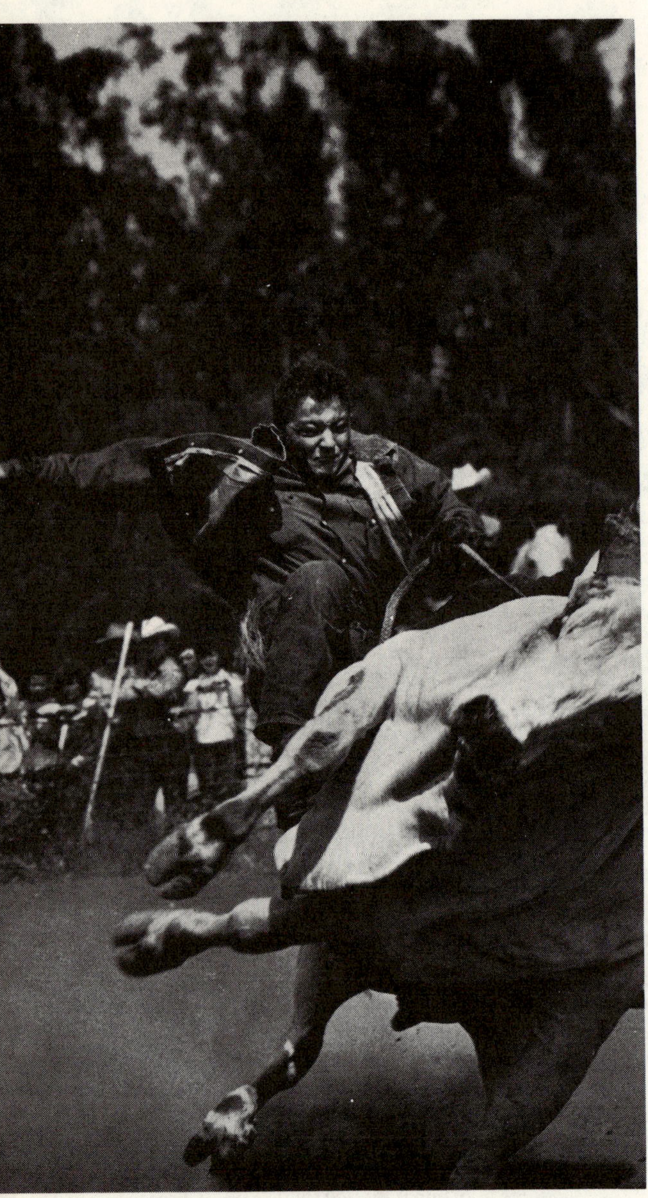

Action photography, which stops action but blurs other areas of the picture to give the feeling of speed, is most effective. Photo courtesy of DuPont.

Another "trick" in stopping action is panning. Preset and focus your camera on the spot where you expect the action to take place. Then, as the subject moves directly in front of you, move your camera with him, clicking the shutter as he reaches the predetermined spot. As you move the camera across, the subject speed is lessened in relation to the camera, and you get a clearer subject, stopped sharply. Remember, with the panning method, the background will be quite blurred. However, this is usually a virtue, since it then appears that the subject actually was moving quite fast.

If at all possible, with stop-action photography, take several shots. At least take similar things, if not always the same thing, so the chance of being able to retain one good photo is heightened. This does not suggest hit-or-miss shooting, but rather advises an inexpensive form of insurance.

CLOSE-UPS

For intimate detail and uncluttered singleness of purpose, close-up photography is the answer. For portraits, nature photography, or other situations where you want your photo to be "right on top" of the subject, try these techniques. Fine close-up photography can be most easily accomplished with interchangeable telephoto lenses. These lenses permit you to select a single face in a crowd, focus, and shoot, capturing it large and clear without the subject's being aware of it.

But close-up photography is not limited to those photographers whose cameras accommodate interchangeable lenses. Just about any camera can be used to take close-ups. The simple box cameras have preset fixed-focus lenses, and as a result, a clear picture can be taken only if you stay beyond the minimum distance—usually five feet. However, add a close-up attachment and you can get closer. Remember, though, the subject will only be clear at the specified close-up range. Take the precaution of using either a tape measure or knotted string to verify the distance from camera to subject, rather than taking the chance of eye-estimating. Remember, also, to shoot slightly above what you see in the viewfinder to allow for the old bugaboo—parallax.

Adjustable cameras make close-up work simpler, since correct range can be checked on the lens' focusing scale. Here, too, close-up lenses and attachments help to further lessen the minimum required distance from camera to subject. To spotlight the subject even more, especially in nature work with flowers, butterflies, insects, and the like, focus critically. The short distance gives a shallow depth of field, so the carefully focused subject "pops out," and the rest of the background is blurred. Here, too, except with the single-lens reflex cameras, which are ideally suited for this type of close-up work, allow for parallax correction. Focus carefully on the subject, then, prior to shooting, lift the camera slightly to allow for the distance between the lens and the viewfinder. Experimentation, practice, and attention to details will result in some beautiful and eye-catching close-ups, with or without a telephoto lens.

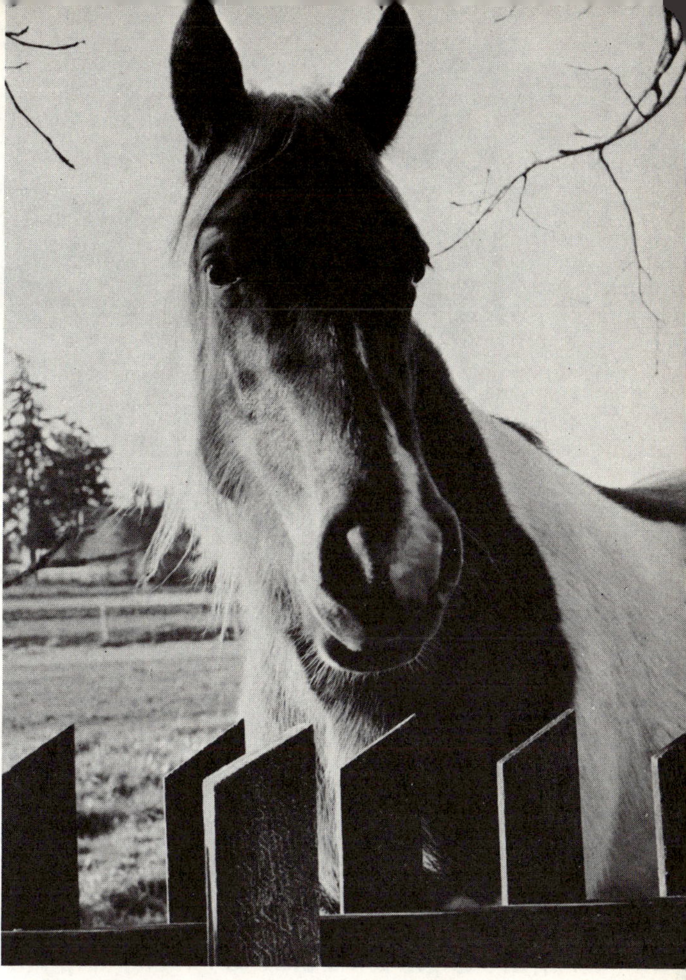

"Friendly," by a 16-year-old amateur, uses lighting to give the photo dimension and undistorted reality. Photo by Glenn Cobb, Jr.

A VARIETY OF VISTAS TO CONQUER

A good photographer, or one striving to become good, rarely misses an opportunity to take photographs. If enough opportunities do not present themselves, he will often set about creating his own opportunities, or at least keeping the possibilities in mind, so when the situations present themselves, he will be ready. It is important, then, that the amateur have a camera fairly accessible to him at most, if not all, times, but especially when he feels good picture-taking situations will occur. Here are a few of these possible situations and what you can do to get good pictures if they suddenly present themselves to you.

On your next airplane trip, you can get spectacular aerial photos if you remember a few simple tips. No matter how clear the day, with either black-and-white or color film, use a haze filter. Focus your camera at infinity, set the shutter speed at 1/100 sec. or faster, and hold the camera steady, close to, but not touching, the window. Take your pictures when the sun and shadows are most dramatic and a feeling of depth can be attained.

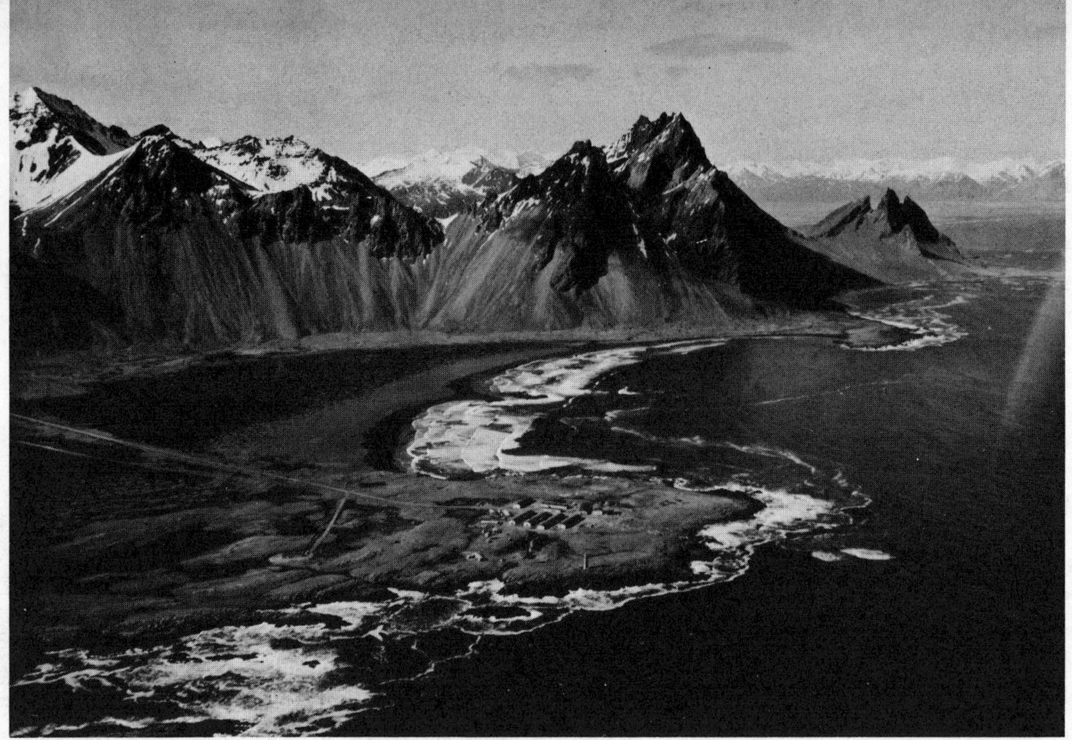

Hofn, Iceland, from the air. Photo by Laurence Van Wallendael.

One of the advantages of having your camera with you at almost all times is that if something happens worth recording, you don't have to be the one left standing forlornly saying, "If I'd only had my camera." Being Johnny-on-the-spot can pay off financially, too. Many newspapers pay handsomely for newsworthy shots. For this type of picture, have your camera loaded with an all-purpose film, such as Plus-X. If you are fortunate enough to be there when something happens, focus quickly, estimate exposure, and take as many pictures of the event as you can, bracketing exposures if possible. If there are people doing a job, such as policemen, firemen, or rescue workers, do not get in their way or in any way make a nuisance of yourself—at this time their jobs are far more important than yours. If you feel you have gotten some good shots, call your newspaper, describe what you think you have in your camera, and make arrangements to turn the film over to them. They will do the rest.

Each of us has seen, and perhaps admired, trick photography. Some of these tricks, perhaps on a smaller scale, can be duplicated by the amateur, and with a bit of imagination, he can even devise his own. One phase of trick photography involves making more than one exposure on either a single negative or piece of printing paper. By selecting a uniform background, and then carefully exposing first the left-hand side and then the right, your subject appears to be in two places at once. If it is done carefully, your subject can even shake hands with himself. To do this with printing paper, carefully mask off first one area and then the other. Use the same lens opening for all exposures, and develop carefully by inspection. Also, by sandwiching two negatives into the enlarger carrier at one time, you can create many interesting shots and effects.

Distance also may be utilized to create amusing effects, since the further away from the camera the subject stands, the smaller he will appear. By having one subject near to the camera and another far away, the nearest subject may even "be pictured" holding an elephant (the farther subject) in his hand.

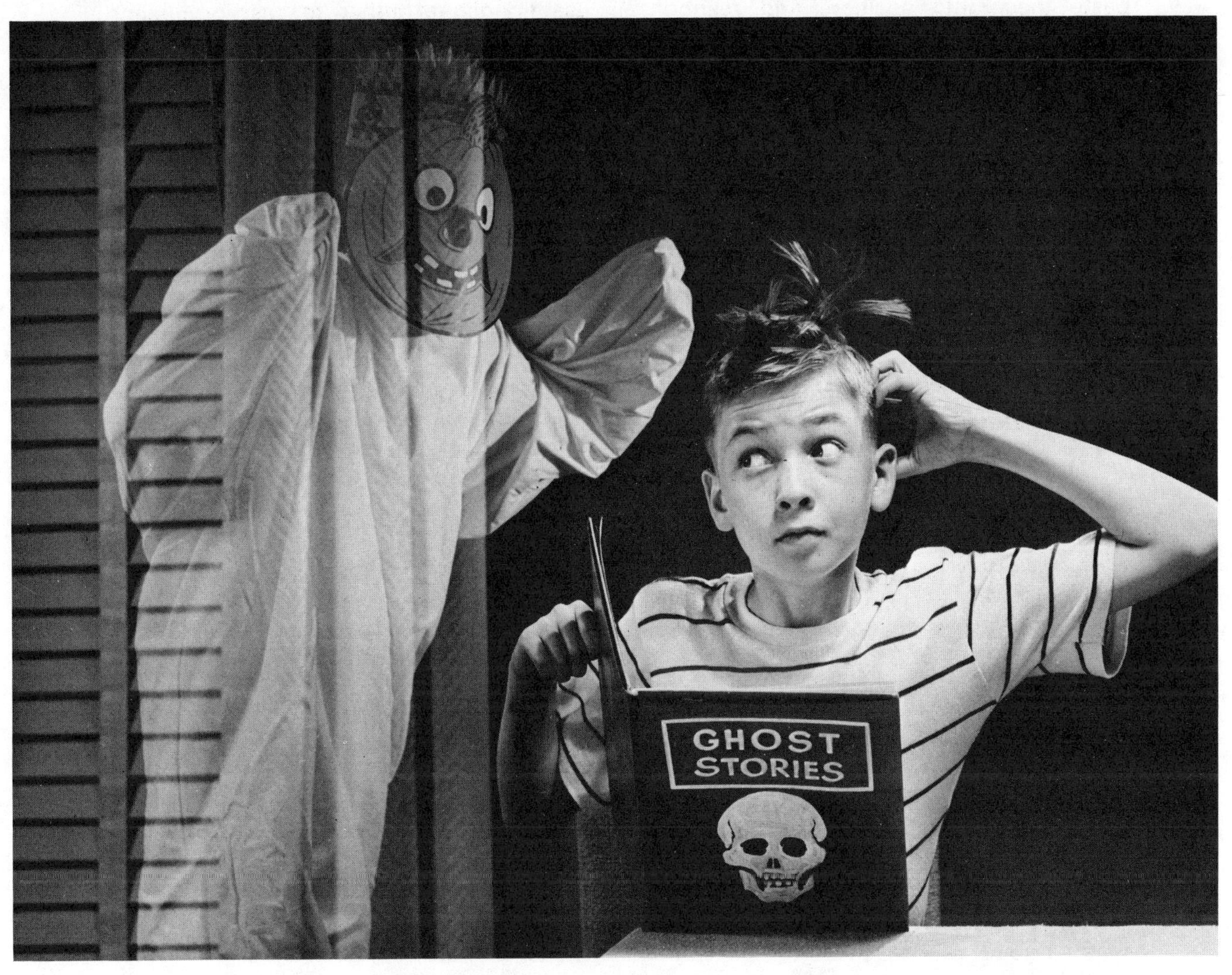

This ghost picture is a simple example of trick photography. Photo courtesy of GAF.

Another trick method involves copying a paste-up. Photograph several elements, paste these into position, and reshoot. Upon printing you will find you have an unusual and different type of photo.

Table-top photography can offer many interesting opportunities for artistic expression, both with the camera and through the use of props and artists' tools and material. Without taking all the pleasure and excitement away from your own ingenuity and imagination, these few examples should help send you on your way. Sugar looks like snow, cotton like clouds, a mirror like ice, carpet like grass, and crumpled paper like water in this creative, imaginative miniatureland. To get better photos of your little scene, make the camera angle work for you. To set a mood, close down the lens as far as possible to give greater depth of field, use floodlights either to cast prominent shadows or eliminate all shadows.

Though a certain degree of realism is desirable when working with table-top units, too much fake realism is likely to ruin a fine effect. Photograph them for what they are, not what they are supposed to be. Ceramic pieces, for example, placed against a cardboard-mounted background, will be much more charming if they look like themselves, rather than if they are faked as real objects. In this field, as in many areas of photography, the product is not only dependent upon equipment and technical skill, but on the taste, imagination, and inquisitiveness of the photographer as well.

Household implements and foods may be arranged to form an attractive still life. Photo courtesy of Agfa-Gevaert.

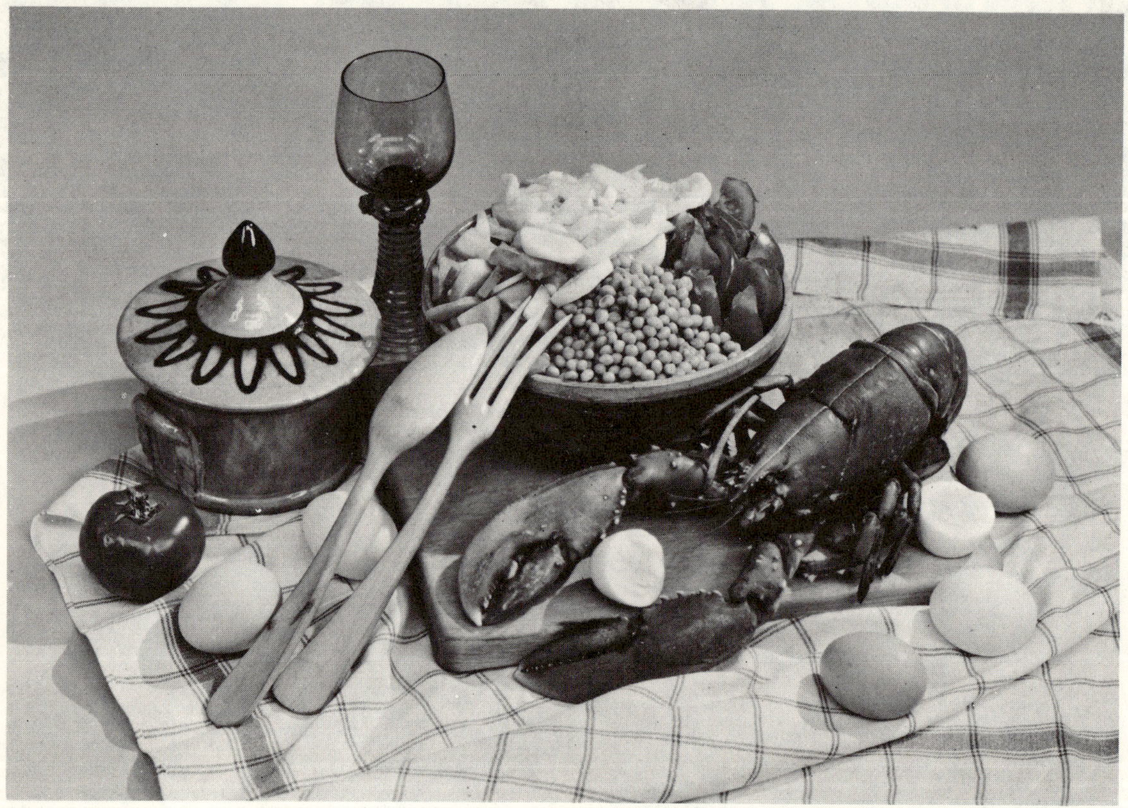

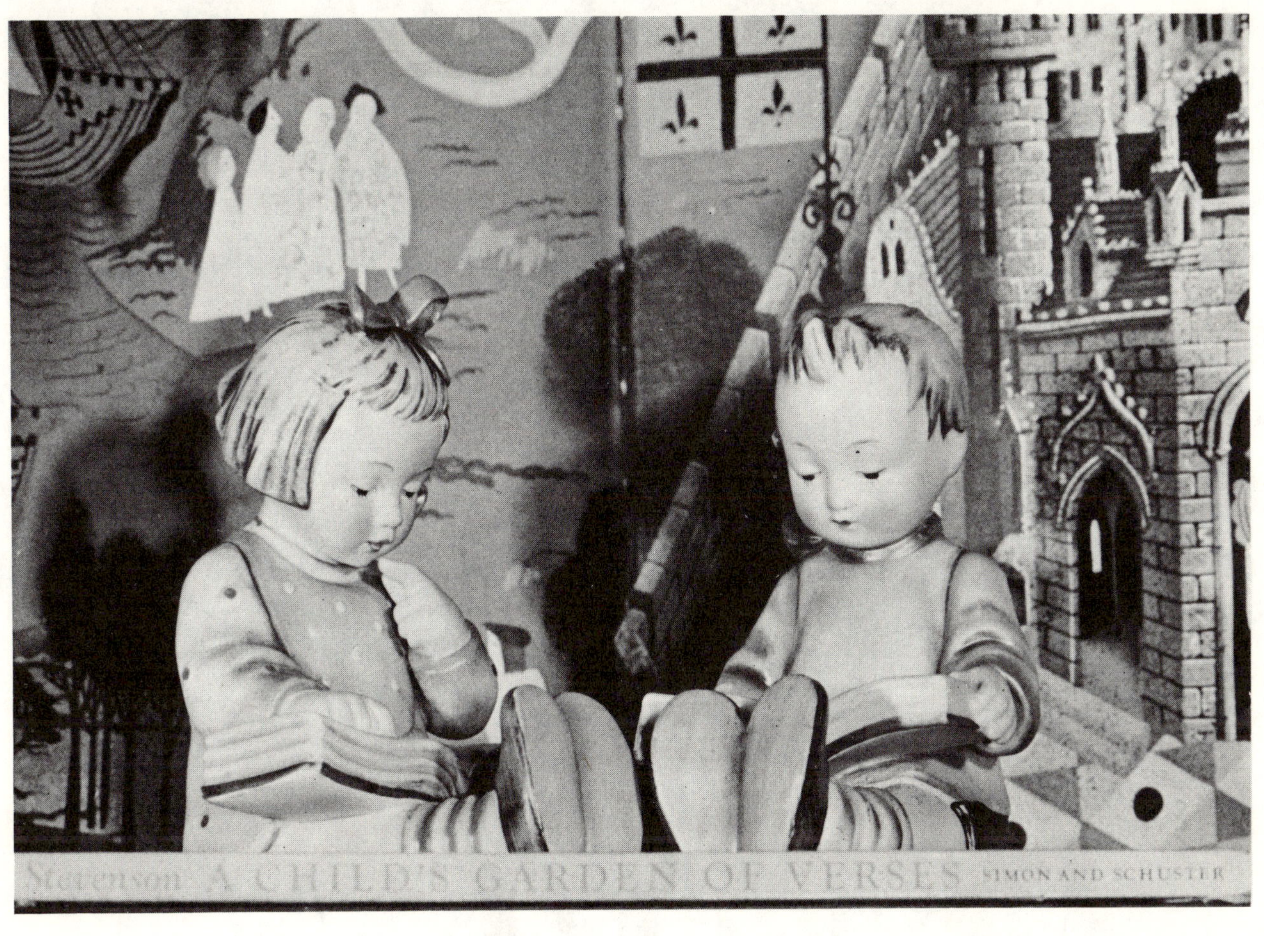

Ceramic figures and an illustrated child's book provide an interesting table-top photograph.
DXF.

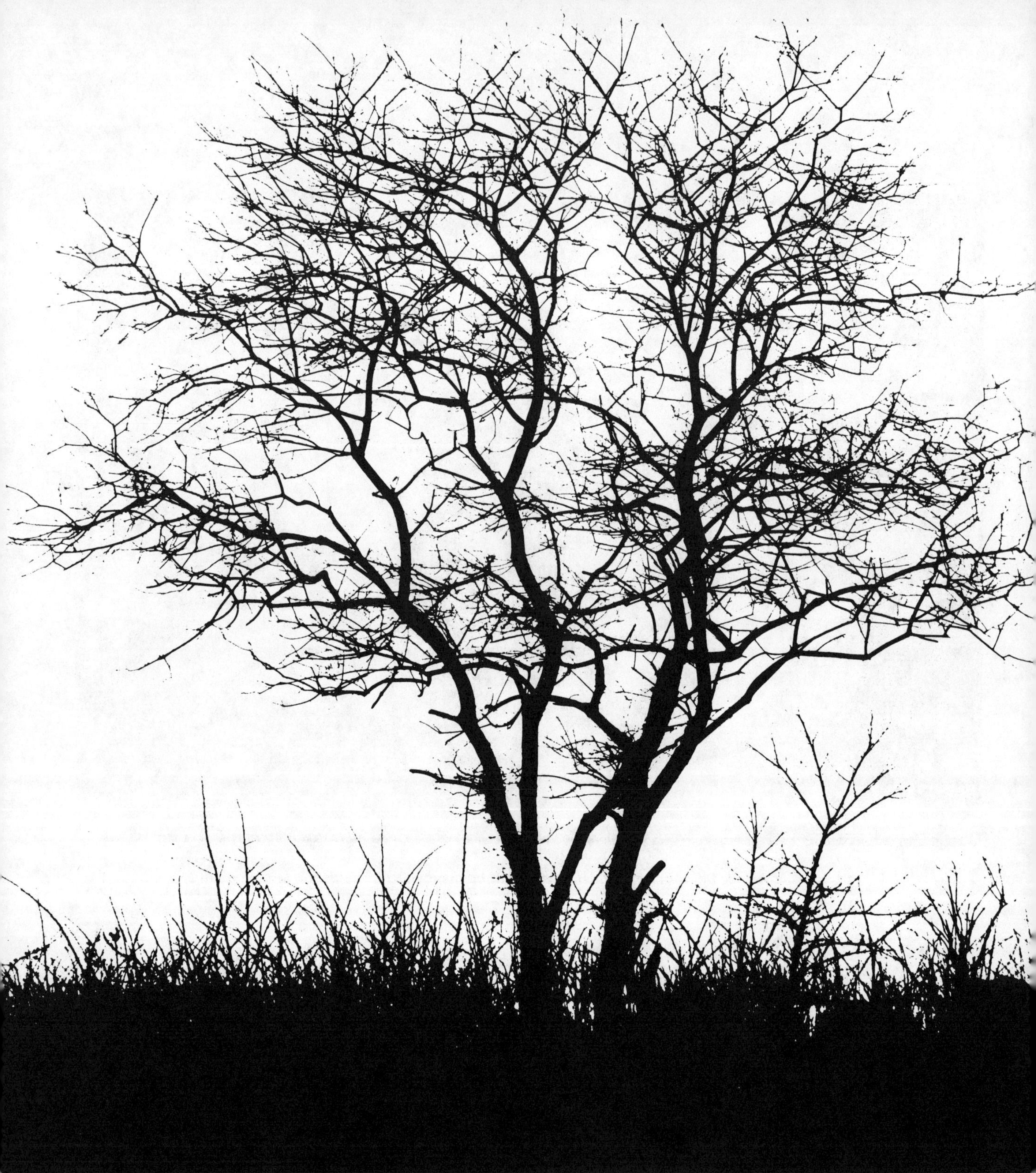

*Darkroom techniques can change ordinary
continuous-tone images into interesting
high-contrast prints. Photo by Herb Taylor.*

9

DARKROOM FACILITY ROUNDS
OUT THE PHOTOGRAPHER

Despite the availability of photofinishing services today, a great many amateur photographers prefer to do their own developing, printing, and enlarging. The reason? Half the fun and excitement of photography takes place in the darkroom as you watch the results of your imagination, talent, and technical skill appear on a piece of paper. So, if you are content to take the snapshot and let the drugstore do the rest, disregard the next few pages. However, if you want additional control over your black-and-white photographic results, the following material should help. Since there are a great many different books currently on the market which explain in great detail how to develop, print, and enlarge, this chapter shall not attempt to compete with these books, but rather will simply present some of the hints, suggestions, and information necessary to help you get better photographs in your own darkroom.

DARKROOM

Some of the most elementary darkroom set-ups allow the production of very fine prints. When purchasing paraphernalia for a darkroom, size, durability, usefulness, and storage compactability are all factors for consideration. One of the best places for an amateur to set up an occasionally used darkroom is the bathroom. The availability of running water, splash- and stain-resistant walls and floor, as well as the probable existence of only a single window make the bathroom fine for a darkroom. For tray developing, or enlarging and printing, a reasonably large, flat, steady surface is required. Depending upon the size of your bathroom you may use a bridge table, ply-wood board, or even an ironing board, to hold trays, enlarger, contact printer, and other equipment. Protect all surfaces with newspaper and then with oilcloth or plastic covering. Of course, if you have a small room at your disposal, a more convenient permanent darkroom can be installed.

Also to be considered when selecting equipment for your darkroom is future expansion as well as present use. Trays should be larger than the largest print you hope to make. Safelights must be chosen according to the paper to be printed, for incorrect safelights will fog certain printing papers. Developers, hypos, short-stops, and printing papers may be selected according to personal preference. Photo stores have large selections made by different companies, and all you need do is decide what you personally wish to achieve. Ask the advice of competent salespeople and try various kinds of darkroom equipment. Recommendations by the manufacturers concerning film-developer combinations, coupled with your own experiments, will give you a head start toward better photos.

DEVELOPING

The step-by-step explanations on film development are easily understood, requiring only some experience and patience. While tray developing is suitable for some of the larger-size films, it is impractical for 35mm films. For 35mm films, tank developing is a must. In learning how to use a tank for film developing, it is imperative to follow the manufacturer's instructions to the letter. The tricky part of tank developing is the loading of the film into the tank in total

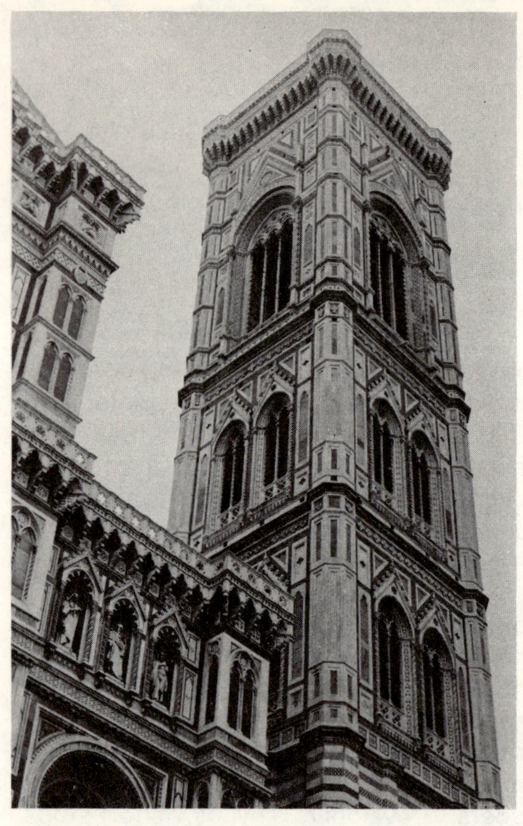

darkness or in a changing bag. Use a dummy roll to practice loading the film, and do it over and over again until you can do it quickly, easily, and correctly each and every time.

For better negatives, and as a result, better prints and enlargements, several suggestions and ideas are offered.

Though it is no longer considered necessary, it does no harm to wash film thoroughly, in water, immediately prior to developing. The washing, in either tray or tank, removes air bubbles, cleans away any unnecessary chemicals, dust, and lint, sets the film for even, streakless development, and makes the film soft and pliable, ready for developing. This rinse bath, which requires only about two minutes, does much to prepare the film for developing as well as to make the job easier for the photographer. Though one can develop film without this pre-rinse, anyone honestly interested in better photos should automatically include it in a processing routine.

For one kind of flexibility, it is a good idea to underdevelop negatives slightly. Most amateurs turn out extremely contrasty or overdeveloped negatives, and these are difficult to soften in printing or enlarging. If, however, the negative is a little underdeveloped and a little soft, it is a simple matter to adjust when printing or developing.

Underexposed negatives, thin or lacking in detail, especially in light areas on the negative, can be remedied through use of an intensifying solution to increase the printing density and negative contrast. For overexposed negatives with dense areas requiring extremely long printing times, reducers will do the reverse job. Do not use intensification or reduction on negatives which are to be greatly enlarged, as these solutions increase graininess. For future avoidance of under- or overexposed negatives, check meter readings carefully and compensate with larger lens opening and longer exposure time for underexposure and the opposite for overexposure.

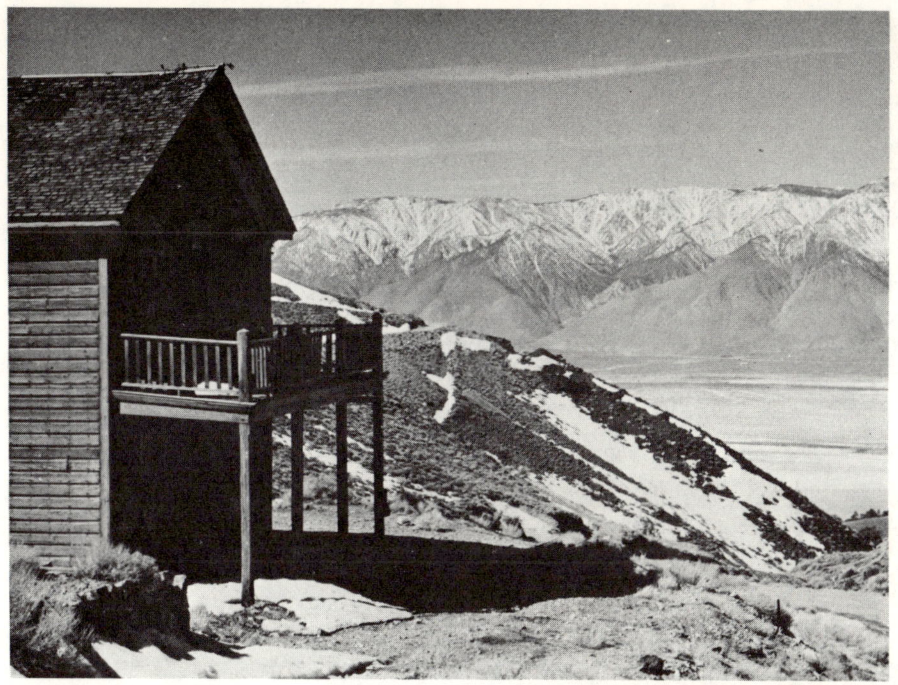

*Allowing for light reflection produces a sharper,
more brilliant picture. Photo by Linda Page.*

Under- or overdevelopment of the negative can result in similar flat or extremely dense negatives. While intensification and reduction may help in these cases, also check to see that all chemicals used for development are at the proper temperature and fresh. When printing underdeveloped negatives, use a contrasty paper, such as No. 3 or 4, and for overdeveloped negatives use low-contrast papers, such as No. 1.

Check your safelight carefully to see that it is color recommended by the film manufacturer. If negatives are the cause of "flat" prints with dense areas and washed-out gray margins, the safelight may be fogging the film. This can also be caused by a too warm developer or one that is incorrect for the film being developed. A quick check of equipment and materials prior to developing, to make sure each is compatible with the others, will repay your few extra minutes with considerably better negatives and prints.

Fixing that has not been completed can cause negatives to turn milky, either overall or in splotches. If you notice this before you expose film to very bright light, put the negative back into hypo for a while. Agitate the film in the fixer to assure all parts being exposed to the hypo. After the prescribed time, they will be completely fixed. Agitation of film plus pre-wetting will also eliminate other negative spots, such as air bubbles. To eliminate the possibility of air bubbles marring the negative, slide film into the developer so all parts of the film are covered quickly and equally.

As is the case with all other phases of photography, care and experience will eliminate many problems and lead you to better photos and more enjoyment. Film developing should be accomplished through a set routine, but it should not become mechanical. Mechanical developing connotes little thought and care, and this type of developing will reward you with poor negatives, and then poor prints and even poorer enlargements. Take pleasure in knowing and doing all parts of photography well, so all steps, from initial exposure to final, mounted print are full of challenge, imagination, and enjoyment.

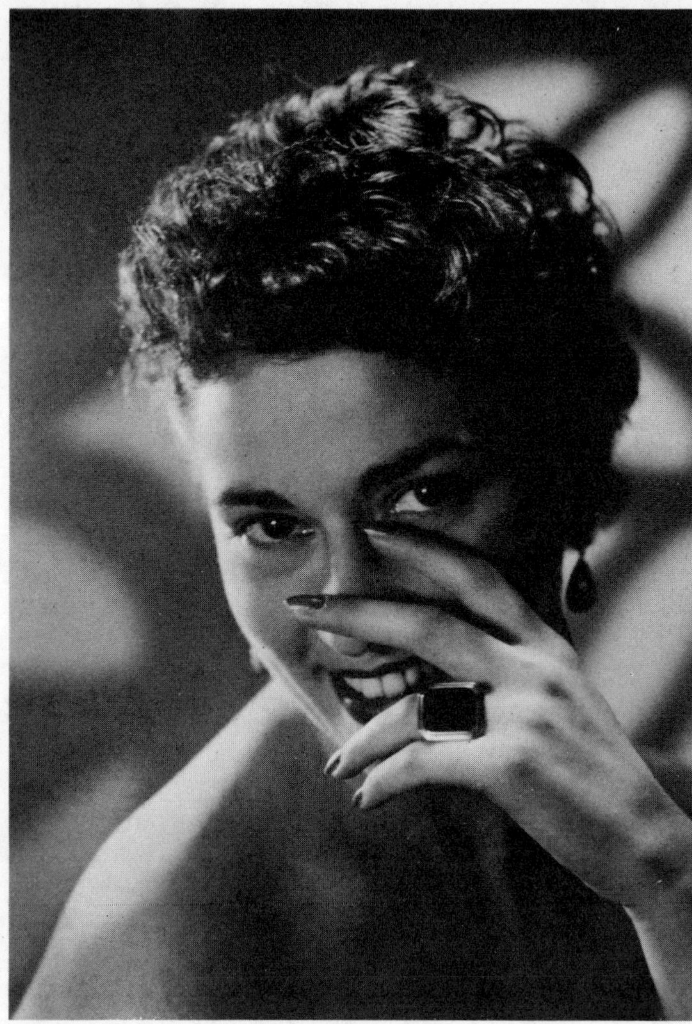

A soft paper can give just the effect desired by the photographer. Photo courtesy of Agfa-Gevaert.

PRINTING

Watching your photo appear as if by magic on a sheet of printing paper is the culmination of all the effort and trials which started when you first decided to take a deeper interest in photography. If you are like most amateur photographers, the moment when your print starts to "come up" in the developer can easily bring one of your greatest thrills in photography.

To get the best from your darkroom and your printing efforts, a small degree of technical skill, learned mostly through experience, is necessary. Most amateurs find they become more proficient in the dark-room as they learn more and more of the "tricks of the trade" and are better able to utilize them along with their own ideas.

Selecting the proper contrast grade of printing paper can go a long way toward helping you get exactly what you are looking for in a print. Numbered from the softest paper, offering least contrast at No. 0 or No. 1, to the contrasty No. 5, the papers must match the contrast level of your negative. A negative considered normal would be best printed on a No. 2 grade of paper, with contrasty negatives on lower numbers, soft negatives on high numbers. Variable-contrast papers, as discussed below, combine several contrast grades in one sheet, by means of filtration during exposure.

76

Varied contrast grades of printing paper are, however, not the panacea for all printing, exposing, and developing shortcomings. For the best prints, and to vary the contrast of the print on a selected paper, vary the exposure time, but keep the development time constant. Upon determining the proper development time from the manufacturer's recommendations and your own experience, stick to it. Change the exposure time to fit the development, for too short or too long a development period will not get the good results a change in exposure time will achieve. In addition, by keeping the development time relatively constant, you are eliminating another darkroom variable with its possibility of error or undesirable effects.

If, therefore, your print is too dark or too light, and your negative is not at fault, you have under- or overexposed the print and should, in making a new print, adjust your exposure, allowing less time for overexposed and more time for underexposed prints, while keeping the developing time constant. Similarly, if the problem is contrast, and your print is too flat with little brilliance, or hard and overcontrasty, change your grade of printing paper to suit the situation. For the flat print, choose a higher numbered, more contrasty paper, and for the hard photo, choose a lower numbered, softer paper.

If your prints develop stains and spots that mar the quality and make the print useless, check your printing and developing technique to eliminate the causes of these errors. Yellow or brown stains are caused by fixing errors, either not enough agitation, an exhausted fixing bath, or incomplete washing. Correct these print ailments accordingly, making sure sufficient time is given in the washing process. The newer resin-coated (RC) papers simplify these procedures considerably.

White spots on a print are caused by air bubbles or by dirt. Air bubbles can be eliminated by sliding the print into the developer tray in such a way that all parts are quickly covered by developer. To remove dirt from print or negative, use a static-free brush or a blower brush. Also, try to keep everything in the darkroom as clean and lint-free as possible. It is infinitely easier to remove dirt and dust spots before printing than to have to laboriously "spot" a print after it has been printed.

Once again, as in developing, a proper safelight plays an important part in printing. The fogging of a print or graying of borders that should be white can be caused by an improper safelight. Each package of paper comes with notes on the safelight to be used with the specific paper. It is wise to follow these suggestions in order to avoid fogged and worthless prints.

Temperature of all chemicals, as well as of washing water, plays an important role in the proper development and processing of a print. Chemical solutions should be kept at a constant 68° F; so should the rinse water. If this is not kept reasonably constant, many flaws will appear on your prints. Not only will the processing be faulty, but your prints may be afflicted with blistering, frilling, and separation of emulsion from paper. In the summer, unless you are fortunate enough to work in an air-conditioned darkroom, you can keep your solutions reasonably constant by placing trays into other trays containing ice water. Keep checking the temperature of the solutions, and when they reach the desired level, do whatever is necessary to maintain this level.

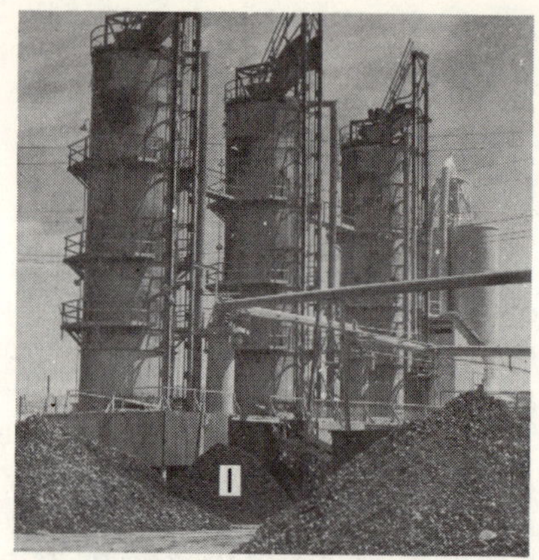

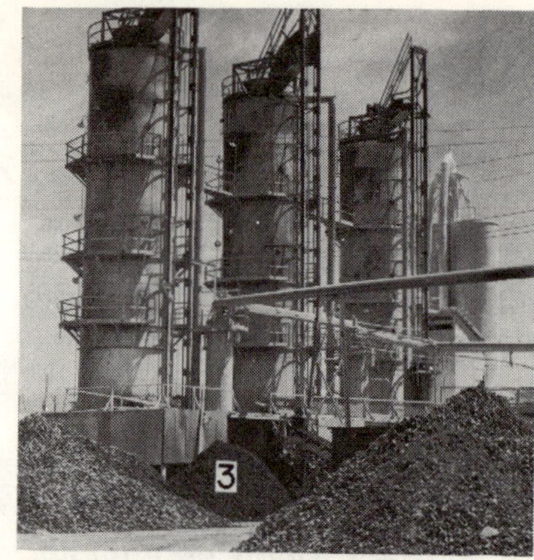

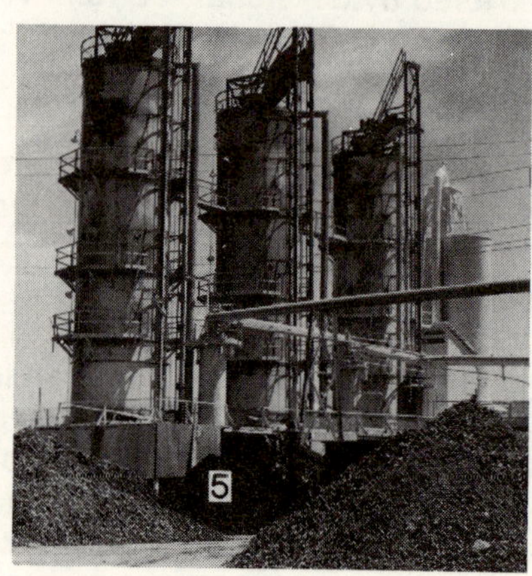

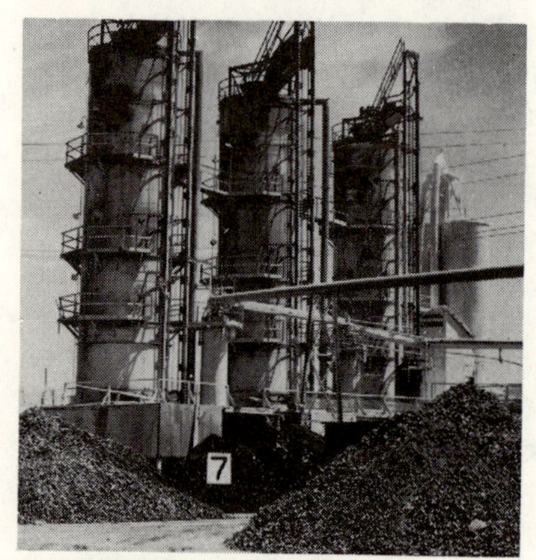

Variable-contrast paper produced this wide variety of contrasts. The numbers indicate the contrast quality of the filters used. Photos courtesy of DuPont.

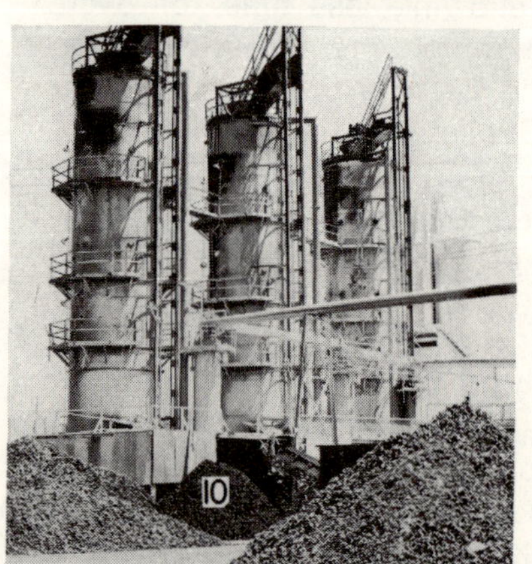

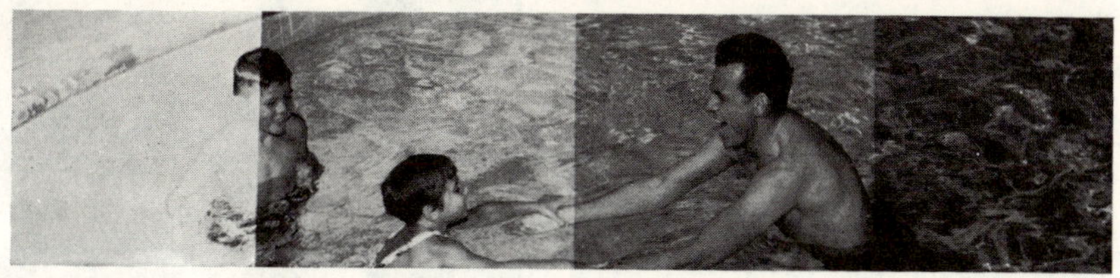

The test strip method of computing exposures saves time and paper by holding make-overs to a minimum. This series, exposed to 4, 8, 16, and 32 seconds, indicates that the 8-second exposure, slightly modified, will produce the best print. Photo courtesy of GAF.

ENLARGING

Any accomplishment requires thought, care, and a great deal of practice. This is true for all phases of photography, especially enlarging. Remember, when enlarging, you are blowing up to large proportions not only each small, good point, but each bad point as well. Care and cleanliness take on new importance when enlarging, or as it is also known, projection printing.

Paper selection is perhaps even more important in enlarging than in contact printing. In addition to the many papers presently on the market in a variety of contrasts and weights, there are also a few that combine many contrasts in a single sheet of paper through the use of filters. DuPont's Varilour, GAF's Vee-Cee Rapid, and Kodak's Polycontrast offer many different contrast levels in a single kind of paper. These papers help solve the problem long fought by the amateur—how to afford to keep many different paper grades and contrasts. A single box of the variable-contrast (VC) paper, coupled with a complete set of special filters, puts the equivalent of a store full of papers at your fingertips.

Enlarger selection should follow careful consideration and considerable discussion with a photo equipment dealer. Both enlarger types, diffusion and condenser, are satisfactory for most applications, but the advantages and disadvantages of each should be carefully examined before purchasing. You will probably have the enlarger you choose for many years, so buy a good one, one that will suit your needs and desires of tomorrow as well as today.

Once you have your equipment and solutions set and ready for use, clean everything in sight—negative, negative carrier, housing, enlarger lens, pressure plate—with either a blower brush or static-free brush. Check and double-check to make certain all dirt, dust, and lint have been removed and will not appear as white spots on a finished print.

To save time as well as paper, when attempting to determine the correct exposure for any given negative, use the test strip method. Make a test strip of exposures at either four- or five-second intervals, of an important part of your photo. Once the correct exposure has been determined, continue to be precise and exact in your timing; better enlargements will result.

Enlarging offers not only a variety of sizes, but the opportunity of selecting that portion of the negative you want, as well as eliminating the unwanted portion. By cropping the print, you point up the most important part of your print, ridding the final picture of any unnecessary distractions or details, producing a more dramatic print. Experimentation, with the negative projected on the printing easel, or on a small contact sheet, will allow you to choose exactly what you want in the enlargement.

Through dodging and burning-in, you can also adjust certain key parts of your enlargement without changing the overall exposure. By dodging, you hold back a portion of the exposure from a certain area, causing it to become highlighted and more

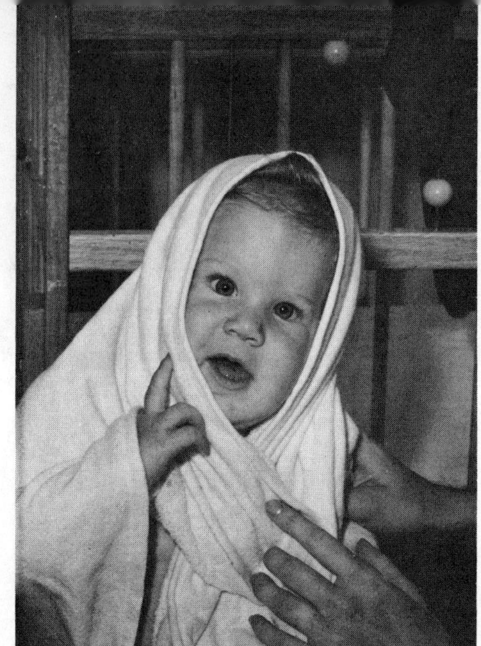

This photo is from an uncropped negative. A more dramatic, cropped version appears on page 50. DXF.

attractive than when darker or excessively shadowed. To dodge, you hold a dodging wand, made of a cardboard disk at the end of a wire, over the area to be held back.

Burning-in is just the opposite of dodging—you allow additional light to hit a specific area, to darken it, while keeping the light from all other areas. A piece of cardboard with a hole in it will serve nicely as a tool for burning-in a section of an enlargement. To control the size of the spot to be burned-in, move cardboard up or down from enlarger, and as with dodging, keep board constantly in motion so no hard edges form. Additional shapes and sizes of holes in cardboard can be used for vignetting and other darkroom tricks. However, it is suggested that darkroom "games" be kept to a minimum, and used only when absolutely necessary and when the photographer has mastered all other facets of darkroom technique.

Darkroom magic need only be limited by the time, patience, and practice you can give to improving your basic developing, printing, and enlarging skills. Once the basics have been mastered, and the spirit of photographic adventure has won you over, a whole new world of enjoyment can be opened for you through experimentation and imagination in the darkroom.

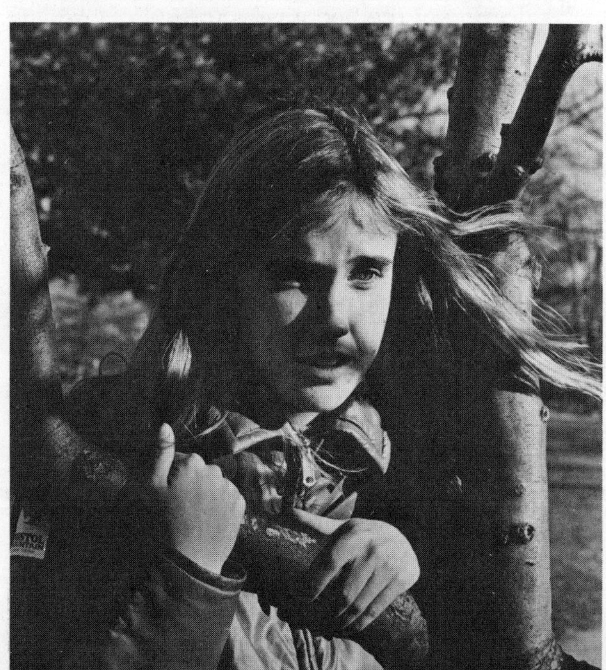

Careful darkroom work turns a good picture into a prizewinner. Photo by Dave Greenwald.

LET PROFESSIONAL JUDGES EVALUATE YOUR WORK

Amateur photography is a field where the doer, the photographer, is usually not his severest critic. The viewing public—be it merely friends or relatives, or thousands of interested spectators—willingly performs this task. The number of exhibitions, contests, and salons indicates that tens of thousands of photographs and slides are viewed by many hundreds of thousands of people each year. This, then, is the amateur's greatest opportunity to have competent professional judges evaluate his photographic efforts, and possibly win an important prize.

To find out the who, what, where, when, and why of contests and exhibitions, the interested photographer need not search very far. Almost all the large photography magazines carry extensive lists, as do the hobby and photography pages of many newspapers. To further supplement this coverage, local camera clubs are sure to have considerable information of their own, as well as of other sponsored contests, and they are pleased to pass on entry blanks and other material.

Since all exhibitions also include many of the elements of a contest—slides and photos competing for acceptance in the exhibition—a definition, or at least a distinction between the two should be drawn. Contests, therefore, will be categorized as those competitions awarding large sums of money or prizes, while exhibitions give medals, ribbons, and a measure of recognition and personal satisfaction.

Photography contests are sponsored by many widely diversified organizations: newspapers; magazines; camera manufacturers; manufacturers of film, flashbulbs, and assorted accessories; and other allied industries and organizations. Prizes in these contests range from token equipment awards to vacation trips to thousands of dollars. The rules are usually quite simple, consisting of submission of a certain number of pictures, taken during a certain period, perhaps on a specific subject. Sometimes manufacturers request use of specific equipment or products. Along with this, the photographer must also submit a complete entry blank, occasionally an entry fee, and the promise of a model release if required.

All photos and slides sent to the contest are judged by competent judges, and winners are announced several months later. You rarely find out how your material rated relative to the other entries, and often don't even have your entry returned. As a result, if you are a winner, you are content to accept the award and consider this the finest contest ever run. On the other hand, if you are one of the many losers, you have lost your pictures and gained nothing, since you don't know, any more than before, just what your pictures were worth.

In direct contrast to the big-paying contests are the no-less-important exhibitions and salons. In these cases, you receive a judge's report card, showing the number of points your entry or entries received, as well as the highest point score possible. There is usually a minimum number of points set for acceptance. Accepted entries are set aside and are judged for medals, ribbons, and stickers.

The photographer, therefore, has a choice. He can either "shoot for the moon," with the big contests, or he can try to achieve a measure of success, recognition, and personal satisfaction from the salons

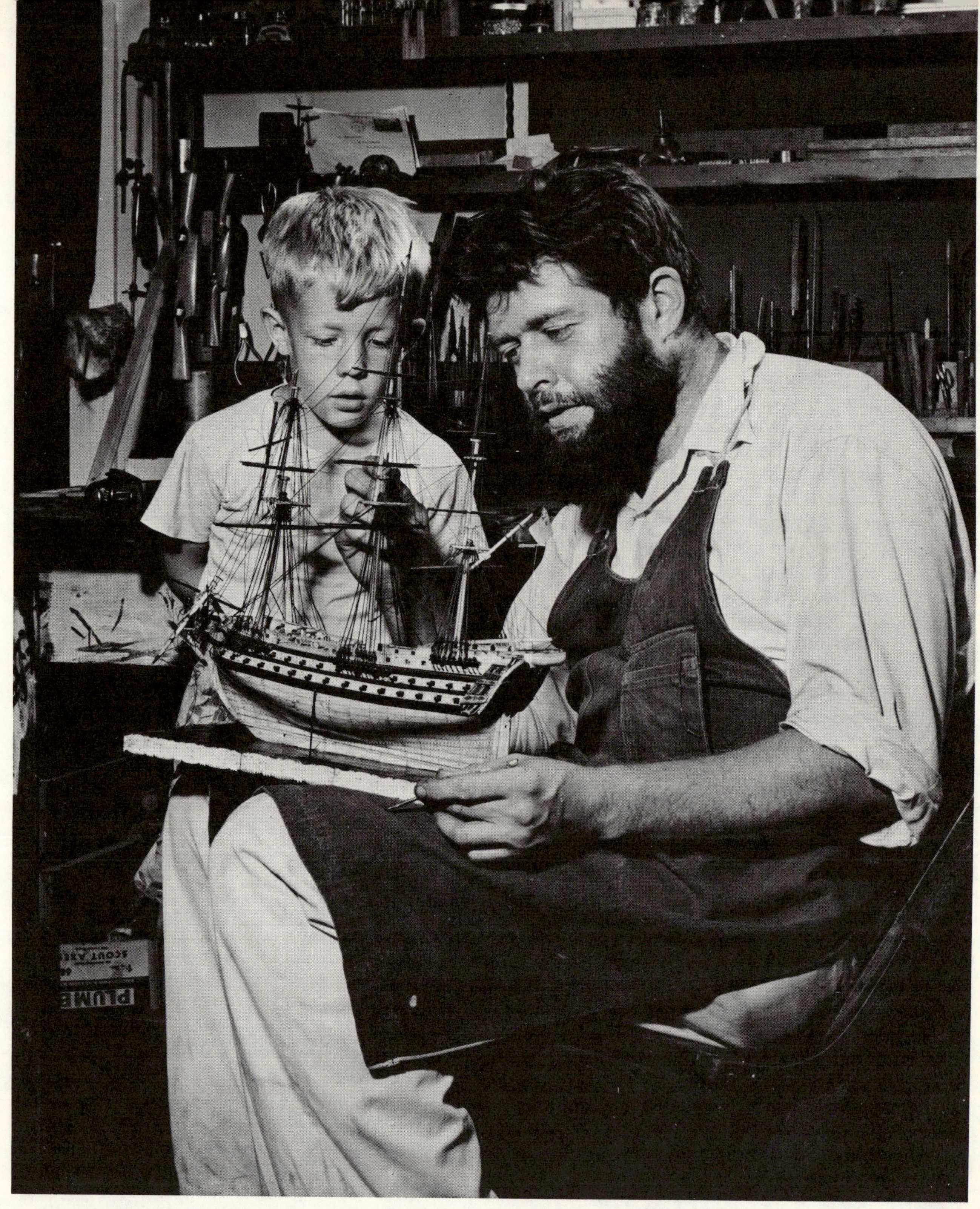

Man and Boy. Photo courtesy of GAF.

and exhibitions. No matter what choice is made, there are several tips and hints which might prove useful in either category.

Most contests and exhibitions ask that black-and-white photos be left unmounted to cut down on the bulk problem in their offices. It is wise to use double-weight paper for these prints, as they hold up better under handling. When mailing these prints, insert them between oversized pieces of corrugated cardboard, with the cardboard ribs running in opposite directions for added protection. Mark the envelope "PHOTOGRAPHS: PLEASE DO NOT BEND" conspicuously, both front and back, and make sure the envelope is well sealed before mailing.

Another problem to be considered concerns the identification of prints and slides destined for judging. A rubber stamp with your name and address, used on the back of each photo submitted, is ideal. If you do not have one, and must use a pencil or pen, use it lightly. A heavy hand behind a pen will dig deeply into the print back, show up on the face, and ruin the entry.

Marking slides poses a different problem. First, determine how they are to be mounted. If mounted for submission in a cardboard mount, you can mark directly on the mount. The glass and metal mounts do not readily accept this treatment, though some metal ones on the market accept inked information. However, for the majority, tiny, printed gummed labels applied to the metal or glass mounts do the job beautifully. If these are not available, small sections of blank gummed labels, with the information handwritten on them, will serve the purpose. Remember, though, this task becomes time-consuming and can be arduous if many slides are entered.

Most organizations also require that slides be "spotted" in the lower left-hand corner, when held in normal viewing position. On cardboard mounts, this spot may be easily applied by touching a small eraser, such as the one on a pencil, to a stamp pad, and then to the slide corner. For metal mounts, a small dab of nail polish will do the trick.

These are a few of the mechanical points to consider once you have made your choice and decided what photos to enter. But, what about the photos themselves? Just what is there about a photograph to make it appeal to a judge and win a prize?

The first quality that makes a photo a prizewinner is eye appeal. A good photo tends to catch the eye and hold it. It makes you want to continue looking at it. This does not mean the photo must be astonishing; rather, it must be something special.

In addition to being eye-catching, it must have universal, or at least, popular appeal. The prizewinner must be something to appeal to many different people with many different tastes. If the situation shown is unique, requiring an explanation for anyone outside your immediate family or neighborhood, the judges will not select it. Keep this in mind when making your selections for submission.

Just about all prizewinning shots are original. They result from a photographer's ideas and emotions and are not merely a copy of another's pose, style, or composition. The judges, as well as the people viewing your entry, don't want to see copies. They have ready access to the originals.

Remember, you are trying to "sell" your entry, and as with any other product for sale, it must look appealing. Don't send the same dog-eared print to a million contests. This isn't appealing in a family scrapbook, so it certainly wouldn't appeal to the selection committee.

Naturally, you will pick the best photos from your collection to submit to any contest or exhibition. Do not send too many entries to a single contest, as several mediocre photos will tend to make the one really good one look like a "fluke." When you decide to enter a contest, don't be slipshod or careless about it. Use a little foresight. Check into the previous contests and winners so you have some idea of what has come before. If you know what the judges want and can supply it, your chances of winning are much greater.

One of the most elementary and important things you must do when entering a contest is to adhere strictly to the rules. This may sound ridiculous to point out and emphasize so strongly, since it sounds so obvious. However, too many amateurs submit material that does not follow the rules, or submit it improperly, and their entries are automatically disqualified. Don't hope that a loose interpretation of the rules will let your pictures be accepted anyway. These pictures probably won't even get as far as the judges. Stick rigidly to the rules, and be sure your prints at least get to be judged.

If your prints or slides are eye-catching, with wide appeal, and are technically sound as well as original, you owe it to yourself to submit them for evaluation by professional judges. Win, lose, or draw, it will give you a better feel of the quality of your photography and perhaps even spur you on to bigger and better things.

"Tracks in the Sand" won first prize for a 15-year-old. Photo by Mark Wilson.

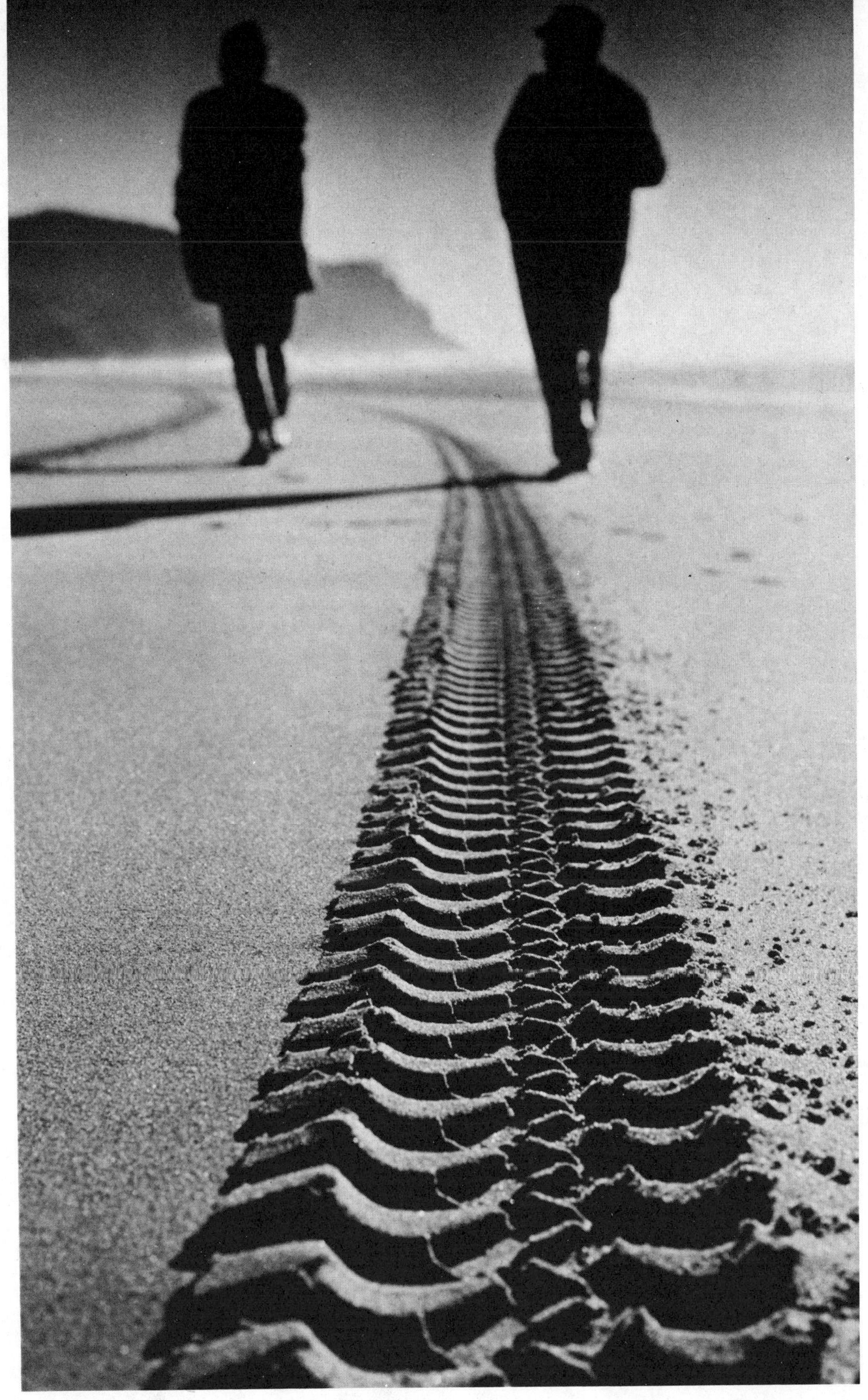

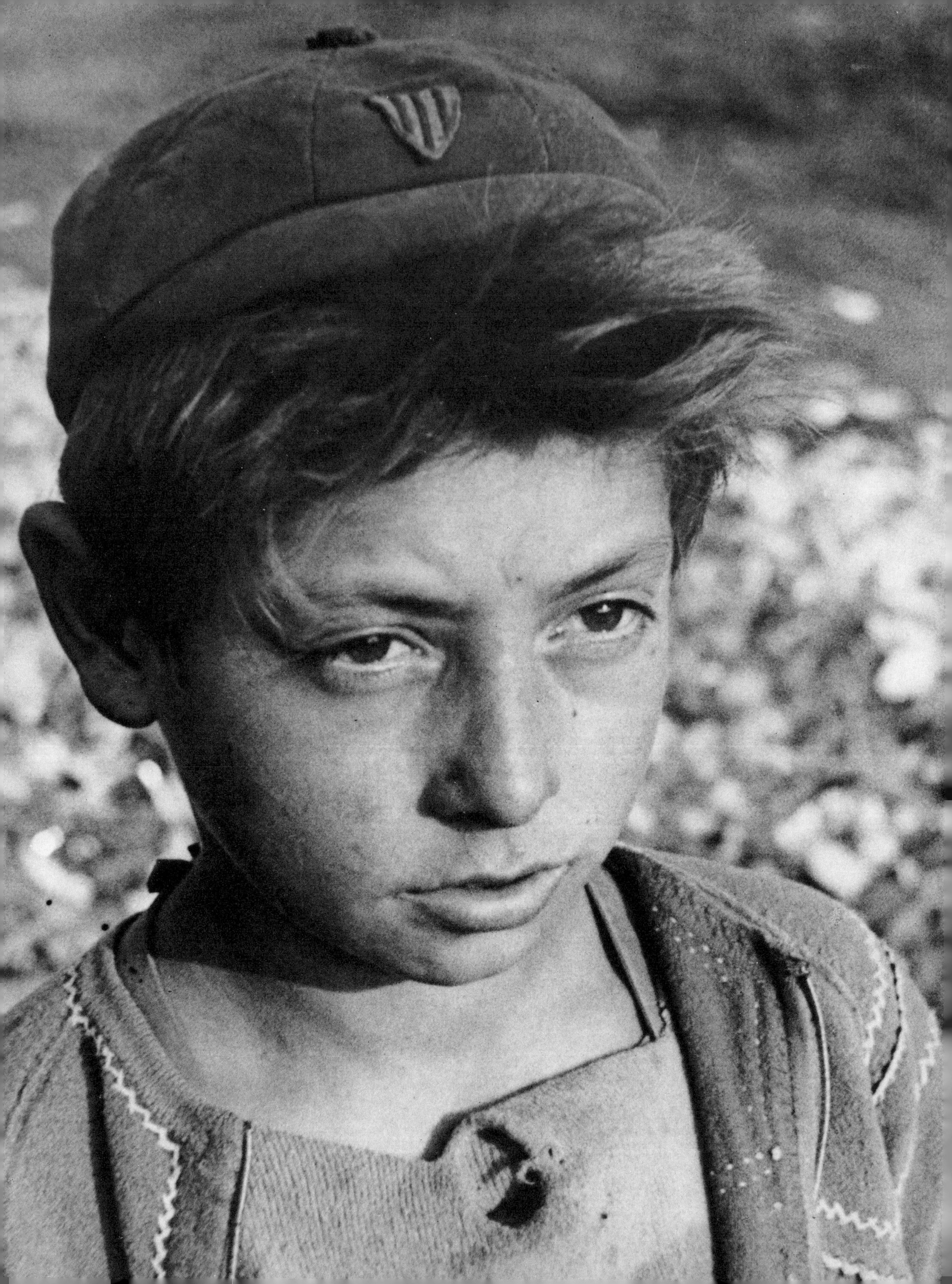

11

THE PROOF IS IN THE PRESENTATION

Photographs are made to be seen. However, this is hard to believe when you see the way many photographers show their pictures. The most dramatic photo loses much of its punch unless it is properly presented. Just as other products need an appealing and interesting package, so does the photographer's product, his photograph. Working on the assumption that a good package makes a fine product look even better, most amateur photographers should hang their heads in shame. They are willing to allow, and even suggest, the showing of their work in a hodge-podge, careless fashion. The photographer owes it to his audience, and certainly to himself and his work, to organize, select, and properly package this "bunch of stuff" and turn it into an enjoyable exhibition of the work he has tried so hard to prepare.

ALBUMS

One of the easiest, and accordingly most popular, methods of presenting a large number of prints is the old-fashioned picture album. On their black pages have been glued, taped, pasted, and cornered, pictorial histories of many families. This method is still quite good today if it is handled in a slightly more modern, diligent, and imaginative manner. The books, which can be kept chronologically or any other way suiting the individual photographer, offer wide format choices and cataloging methods: white ink, poster paint, or typed labels used for captions greatly enhance presentation, while explaining and describing people, places, and things.

While this album method is adequate, it is little more than that. It is not very special. Each of us has a few extra-special negatives about which we are particularly proud. They should not be snowed under, or hidden away in an already overloaded family album. These negatives should be used to make enlarged prints—prints large enough to really do the photo justice. Fine enlargements from small negatives can be made as large as 8″ x 10″, 11″ x 14″, and even 16″ x 20″. Once made, these prints must be preserved and displayed to fulfill maximum satisfaction.

If you are fortunate enough to have many of these extra-special prints, they should naturally be kept together—weddings, parties, baby's first year—and should have an extra-special album. Select the very best of these special prints, mount them, and put them into a presentation binder. These binders, which can be loose-leaf or spiral-bound, lend themselves to imaginative decoration as well as the freedom of adding, rearranging, or removing. Covers may be lettered, pages identified, and the book generally "prettied up" so your album takes on the look of a professional presentation. Select a book that comes with plastic folders over each page to protect the prints against dirt, dust, fingerprints, and other things which might spoil the enjoyment of your prints in years to come. You see, if they are special, many people will want to see them.

Urchin. Photo courtesy of GaMi.

MOUNTING

Often, we have one very special print which we would like to mount, mat, and display on a wall in our home. There are many different ways to mount enlargements, all adaptable for wall or album presentation. The easiest way is to coat the back of the print and the mounting board with rubber cement, and when both are dry, apply one to the other. The mounting board used for photos is a special two-layer cardboard, available at art supply stores. To avoid having air bubbles form underneath the print, do not try to mount the entire print at one time. Instead, touch the top of the print back to the top of the pre-glued board. Cover the print with tissue paper while working with it, in order to protect it properly. Slowly and carefully, work the print down from the top point with your palm, moving it in a circular, downward motion. This method is adequate, but not permanent, and should be avoided for your best prints.

An equally simple, but more professional mounting method uses mounting tissue and heat to attach the print to the board. The mounting tissue is a waxed paper, coated and containing adhesive on both sides, which sets when heat is applied. To mount, the tissue should first be cut to the approximate size of the print to be mounted. Using either a specially made tacking iron, or an ordinary home pressing iron, tack the tissue to the print at one corner. Place the print under a sheet of brown wrapping paper and again apply a small amount of heat to a corner or edge to tack the print into position on the mount board. With the brown paper over the print to protect it, apply heat and pressure to the photo. Do not linger in any one spot too long or use too hot an iron, as either will cause the print to turn brown or burn. If you have access to a dry-mount press, the exact heat and pressure can be regulated. However, by using a household iron carefully, and keeping it moving continuously while applying pressure, a creditable mount may be made. With resin-coated and color-print papers, *great* care must be exercised to prevent damaging the print. Exact time and temperature suggestions will be found on the mounting-tissue package.

To mat or frame your photos, mount first as previously explained, and then add an appropriately cut and sized mat frame. While most photographers make the bottom margin of the mat slightly larger than the top one, this is entirely up to the taste and discretion of the photographer. To cut the hole in the mat, through which the photo is to be viewed, measure the total picture area of the photograph, allowing about $1/8''$ on each side, and carefully cut to size. Apply rubber cement to the mat and the mount as previously described. Place the mat atop the already mounted picture, apply pressure, and keep weighted for a period of time.

Pictures prepared in this manner, with mount and mat, may be displayed in many different ways—within frames, in frameless hangers such as Bracquettes, on easels, peg boards, and almost every other conceivable method of exhibition. In whichever way the photos are used or shown, the photographer is assured his prints are being presented at their very best, and are being protected at the same time.

SLIDES

How many times have you been a captive audience at the slide show of some relative or friend? Invited under an entirely different guise, you suddenly find yourself in the middle of "this new batch of slides I got back yesterday." And that's just how they go into the projector—disorganized, unplanned, uncoordinated, and uninteresting.

Anyone who has ever endured one of

these tests of tact and diplomacy should understandably want to avoid making the same mistake. For good slide shows, and the opportunity to have your guests ask to see your latest slides the next time they visit, a few rules must be followed:

1. When slides are returned from the processor, go through them with a hand viewer, and discard those that are, for one reason or another, unshowable or duplicated.

2. After you have eliminated the really bad slides, select those of interest only to you and your immediate family. Put these away as personal slides, to be viewed only by those concerned.

3. From the remaining slides, choose those technically best, and of interest to the widest group of people. These should be categorized and put in order, then placed into holders or magazines for projection.

4. To the excellent slides, suitable for public showing, you should add appropriate title slides. They add immeasurably to the show, with both informative and visual appeal. You can either make these title slides yourself, or buy the ones which are already for sale in stores. They should be short and to the point, which is more than can be said for most oral explanations by the photographer.

TITLE SLIDES

These slides, which may be as simple or as complex as the photographer's talent and imagination allow, should accompany every set of slides shown that normally requires some discussion at beginning or end. While an explanation of how to make title slides does not really tell you how to take better photos (the avowed aim of this book), it will show you how to make your better photos look even better.

Some of the best title slides simply utilize existing landmarks or signs. Others may be made "to order" for one specific set of slides. The latter are especially good, and show the imagination and skill of the photographer.

To use existing scenery, landmarks, or signs for title slides, select the ones you want, and shoot. If they are not sufficiently explanatory in themselves, and you wish to add a date or other information, place plastic letters on a sheet of glass or clear plastic, hold them in front of the camera, adjust the camera for maximum depth of field, and shoot. Other title slides may be adapted from picture postcards with type attached, or from maps with appropriate lettering and props.

If you are so inclined, any picture or lettering you can devise will make excellent, personal title slides. Those of us who lack artistic talent ourselves can do just as well with a little imagination, a glue pot, and a pair of shears. By clipping an appropriate illustration from a magazine, and adding letters available at art and photo stores, you can make a fine title slide.

A few cautions must be observed when using some of the aforementioned suggestions for making title slides. When using glass or plastic to hold the lettering, reflections may become a problem. By tilting the glass slightly forward, the reflections will be eliminated. Plastic lettering has little depth, and is available in several colors, making it ideal for title slides. The glossy shine, which can cause reflections, can be eliminated by spraying the lettering with plastic dulling spray. With lettering sets whose letters have depth, such as cork or plaster of paris, have lighting come from only one direction, upper left, for the shadows from several light sources will make the lettering difficult to read. These suggestions, plus your own experiments and experiences, will teach you how to get better title slides and thus, better slide shows.

COLOR ENLARGEMENTS

Since fine color prints and enlargements can be made from both color negative and reversal type film, they should be considered not only for snapshots, but for exhibition purposes as well. The same procedures for mounting, matting, and display should be followed as outlined for black-and-white prints and enlargements. However, with color, extreme caution should be exercised to follow precisely the manufacturer's advice concerning the application of heat and certain adhesives. As a general rule, less heat should be used on color prints and enlargements than on similar black-and-white prints. In addition, certain adhesives will cause discoloration on color prints, and should therefore be avoided.

It is extremely important, therefore, that amateur photographers improve not only their techniques of picture-taking, but of picture presentation as well. As the photos improve, so must the method of display.

An out-of-the-ordinary shot can "make" a vacation album. Photo by Dave Greenwald.

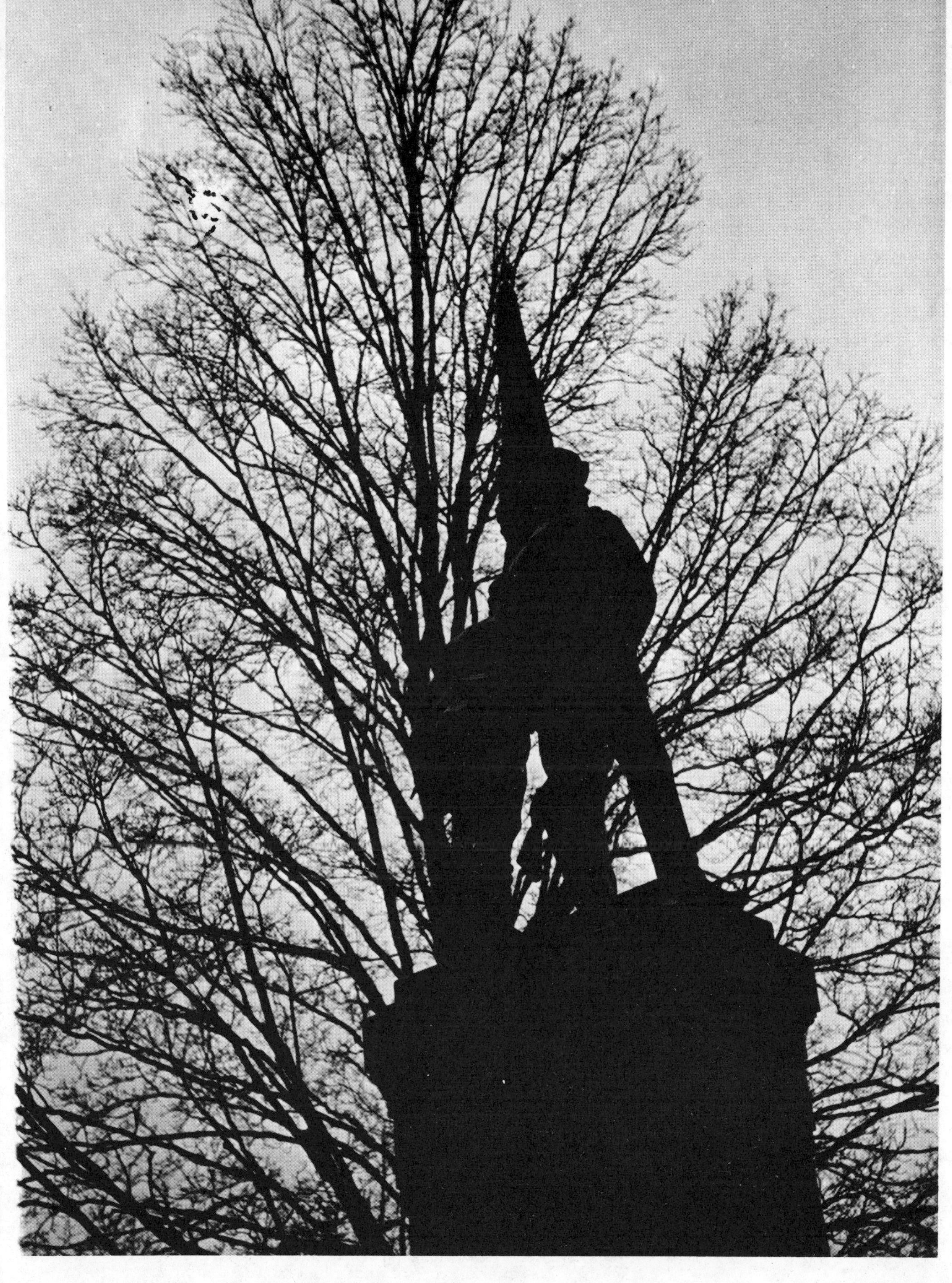

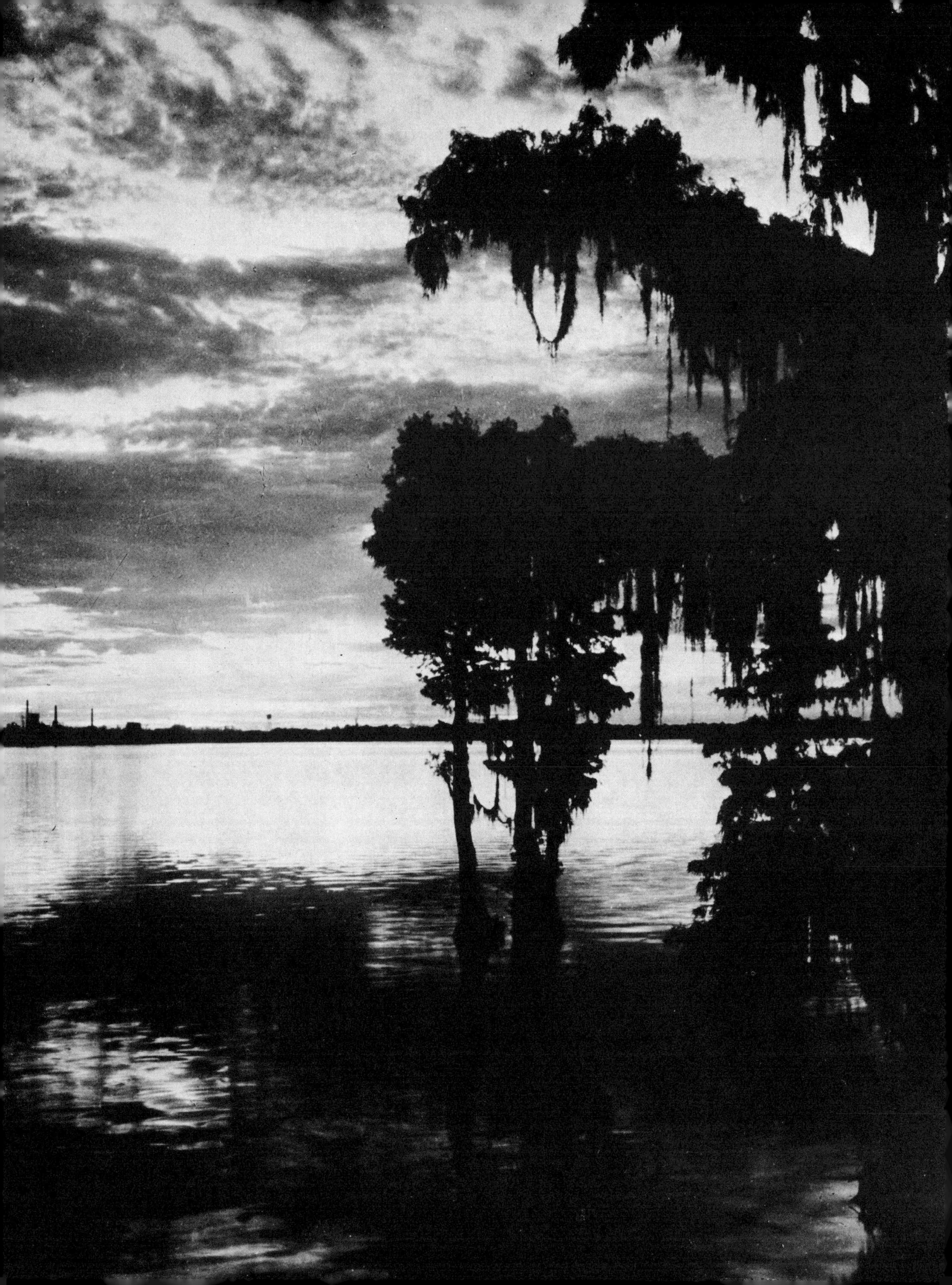

12

AND SO . . .

Amateur photography requires a bit more than the optimistic camera advertisements try to make you believe. In writing this book, we have tried to make amateurs realize that while photography is not a difficult art, neither does it merely consist of camera, film, and a click of the shutter button.

Photography's technical side can be learned by anyone with a genuine desire to master its reasonably uncomplicated but strict set of rules and regulations. There is a great deal of latitude within most facets of this technical part of photography, so that often an error made at some point of the picture-taking operation may be corrected at the picture-making end. It is, therefore, extremely beneficial for the amateur photographer to do all of his own photography, from picture-taking through developing, printing, and enlarging. For in this way, and in this way alone, will he be able to learn, observe, and gain the necessary experience to take and make better photographs.

It is not, however, the technical part of photography that is, at least to me, the most important part. For what good is a print that has been perfectly exposed, accurately developed, and carefully printed if the subject is nondescript, or if the composition is just plain bad? We have noted that photography is an art, and as a recognized art form it must be creative rather than merely reproductive. The amateur should strive to record on film a small part of his inner self. Each of us has a certain measure of creativity, most times dormant, which should be brought to the surface if the photograph and photographer are going to amount to much. It is this creativity, coupled, of course, with the technical knowledge required to take the picture properly, that can make the difference between a picture and a beautiful photograph.

If the amateur photographer can remember to see things not just as the physical things they are—cars, trees, people—but as a small part of the symphony of living, he can translate his thoughts and creative ingenuity to the camera's canvas, film. He must see beauty. He must realize that the commonplace things about him, as well as the so-called beautiful ones, all contain a certain measure of beauty. Just as a child must crawl before he can walk, so must the photographer see before he can record.

This book, like so many before it, and many still to come, serves only a single purpose—to excite the amateur photographer into taking better photographs, and as a result, give himself more enjoyment. To do this we have tried to explain and simplify, with hints and suggestions, the varied facets of photography so these picture-taking requirements can become second nature, and allow additional time and thought for better and more creative photography.

In the final analysis, better photography is not up to the camera, the developing, the printing, or any one of the technical processes, though they certainly do help. It is up to the photographer, with the eyes, brain, and imagination to capture something beautiful, something that has a creative beauty shining out for all to see. The amateur photographer can achieve this, if he will only look.

Morning Fog. Photo by James V. Schildgen.

ACKNOWLEDGMENTS

A book on photography would be nothing without pictures, and an amateur photography book would be less than honest without fine amateur photos. The author, therefore, gratefully acknowledges the contributions of many photographers and organizations whose works illustrate this book.

Special thanks are due the Eastman Kodak Company for the use of the prizewinners in their Kodak High School Photo Contest: "Industry," "Tracks in the Sand," "The Ayes Have It," "Friendly," and the portrait by Sven Kado; to Graflex, Incorporated, for use of the winning pictures from the 11th Annual Graflex Photo Contest: "Morning Fog," "Hay Time," "The Yawn," and "Boating Westward"; to E. I. DuPont de Nemours for their lighting photos and rodeo action shot; to the Polaroid Land people for "Nantucket" and the night shot by Nick Dean, and to GAF for their many photos. And, of course, to Linda Page, Dave Greenwald, and Greg Miller for photos that should be the start, with many, many more sure to come.

INDEX